three days to eternity

BEING THE STORY
OF FATHER   CAIRNS,
MARYKNOLL   ONER
AND MODER   STLE

by Richard Reid ... *rd J. Moffett*

THE NEWMAN PRESS
Westminster, Maryland, 1956

NIHIL OBSTAT:
John A. Goodwine, J.C.D.
Censor librorum

IMPRIMATUR:
✠ Francis Cardinal Spellman
Archbishop of New York

The nihil obstat and imprimatur are official
declarations that a book or pamphlet is free of
doctrinal or moral error. No implication is contained therein that those who have granted the
nihil obstat and imprimatur agree with the contents,
opinions, or statements expressed.

Library of Congress Catalog Card Number: 56–13467
Copyright, 1956, by
The Catholic Foreign Mission Society of America,
Maryknoll, N.Y.
Printed in the United States of America
by H. Wolff, New York

In sacred and glorious memory of
those Chinese who
in our day have shed their blood
for God and China

contents

three days to eternity

PROLOGUE : **memories**

His name was Cairns.
His address, China.
His profession, apostle.
His triumph, martyrdom.
His grave, the China Sea.

This story of the life and death of Father Robert J. Cairns, Maryknoll Missioner, begins three days before his eternity.

It begins half a dozen days after the Japanese attack on Pearl Harbor. It begins on Sancian Island, that little clump of grassy rock jutting out of the sea, six miles off China's southern coast.

It begins on the raw, December afternoon when a Japanese Army colonel told a Maryknoll missioner that he must flee or die.

It starts on the day Father Sandy Cairns made his decision to stay with his flock come torture or death.

It's the seventy-two hours in which the memories of a man's life crowd in upon him before he, the good shepherd, lays down his life for his sheep.

It's the story of the three days before Father Robert J. Cairns began his eternity—the triduum of his Gethsemane, his journey to Calvary, and his crucifixion.

It's the story of the flashback of a hard and holy life, which ended in triumph and glory in the arms of the Queen of Martyrs.

So, in a little mission hut on the side of an island mountain, looking out across the water to the China mainland, let us be with Father Sandy and swing back through the years with him in recollections of the paths and byroads of a life that led him on to the summit of heroic death.

There will be the wet, shiny cobblestones of Glasgow's soft morning. The excited hour when a mother and her brood dock at Boston and rush into the arms of a waiting Scottish husband and father. Together we'll go back to the streets and scenes of turn-of-the-century Worcester, Massachusetts. To the pranks and prayers of a little boy's growing up. To the soccer field, the parish sacristy, and the corner candy store. The tin-whistle days when a freckle-faced youngster played and clowned his way into the hearts of half a city. We'll buy the evening paper from a newsboy who has begun to dream of bringing other news to the ends of the earth.

If we reminisce with Sandy, we'll live again with him the happy hours at Holy Cross College. There'll be the tug and pull of a pretty Irish face, on the heartstrings of a lad who was made to love. Then the hushed weeks of wonder when a Catholic boy wakens to the challenge of Christ's army, daring to dream of the priesthood. The thrill and throes of the big decision. Then the bells and books and the long years in the seminary—St. Mary's, Baltimore. The reckless drive to give more and more to God. The vision of a billion people without faith, or hope, or love. The foreign missions.

We'll go with Sandy to volunteer for battle on the front lines. To the newly founded American Foreign Mission Seminary at Ossining, New York. Through the hidden life of training of 'another Christ'—of a wandering one. Then the delirium of joy and power and trembling of ordination day. A kind of pride and humility all mixed up in glory, exploding inside of him. We must wait with Father Sandy through the dragging, anxious months till that electrifying moment when the words "To China" light a fire to roaring in his very soul. To the pagan world. To the poor and the sick and the despairing. To the rice fields, to the famines and floods of the Orient. To the Chinese millions not yet knowing that they yearn to love and be loved by the God-man who died on a cross to save their souls.

The memories of the first years among his adopted people will come to life again for Father Sandy, and through him for us. The remembrances of trying to coax and tease the singsong of the Cantonese language into his eager head. The long treks over hot mountains and through steaming rice paddies to take Viaticum to a dying convert. The unending hours of catechizing South China's farmers in the Creed, the Commandments, and the consolations of our holy Faith. The hungry days. The torrid weather. The sting of fever. Yet always and ever the sustaining, holy wonder at his harvest of souls for God.

Thoughts run back to the final phase of his apostolic career. His assignment to Sancian—as successor to Francis Xavier. A field of his very own, for sowing love and reaping souls. The sad-happy weariness of bringing up a people in the image and ways of God. The frustrations and the victories. The suffering and the thrills. The glorious, happy humility of being 'father' to his Christians. Of being shepherd to his sheep. Of being lover to his Beloved.

The crowding in on us, in the togetherness of the memories we are sharing, of the first bursts and brutality of war. Father Sandy's calming hand on panicked brows. His fearless faith supporting all on his island kingdom. The landing of Japanese troops. His brave, inviting call to each and every sacrifice. His worry for his flock. The threats. The bombs. The bullets. Then the final warning—"Flee or die!"

Why, that was only yesterday.

Tomorrow, the crown.

But today, memories.

. . . of Scotland

Long years ago, about three quarters of a century now, a son was born to a Scottish miner. This miner, Robert Cairns, came of a Catholic family whose ancestors a generation before had fled the Penal Laws in Ireland to make a new life in free, if Calvinistic, Scotland. There Irish immigrants could have their priests to warm their hard, poor lives lived out in voluntary exile for the Faith.

Of such a stock and breed was miner Robert. The Irish heritage of the new Scots put sense and grace into careers destined for hard work, big families, and border poverty. This lad early went to dig in the mines that bordered Glasgow—gaping pits edging into the very limits of the city's poorer neighborhoods and making them poorer still. Robert worked to help his parents, to lighten the load of a large and growing family.

But the day comes, in the working life of a young man, when he feels the need of a home and family of his very own. Robert Cairns, miner's son and miner, fell in love with a Scottish lass, Janet Allison, in the spring of 1874. After a year-long, stormy courtship—for Janet's father was a staunch and determined Protestant—Robert and Janet wed, on July 5, in his parish church in Glasgow's Irish quarter, New Kilpatrick Village.

The couple lived on love, and hardly anything more, in a small house close to Robert's mine. In the spring following their wedding, sorrow brought Robert and Janet even closer together. Their first child, Thomas, died at birth. A little girl came next, christened with the name of her young mother. She was as strong and straight as any lass in Scotland. The joy of the Cairns was full.

The next year, Helen was born. Then Agnes, in 1880. Robert and Janet longed for the blessing of a son. Their prayers were triply answered in 1881, 1882, and 1884, when the parish priest baptized James, Archibald, and Robert in that order. So, here was Sandy, born August 21, 1884, and christened as Robert John, a few days later in St. Patrick's Church, Glasgow.

This little fellow so crowded the growing family that the parents decided to move to a house with a larger kitchen and more room for the multiplying cots. Soon after the family had settled in their new and larger home, the father realized that he could never adequately fill the needs of his wife and six young ones on the wages from the mines, where advancement was slow and pay-raise rare.

In a bold moment, built up by months of prayer and planning, the father made the plunge. He quit the mines, rented a shop, and went into the dry-goods business. It was a tremendous venture for a young man who had spent his teens and the early years of his fatherhood in the bottom of a Glasgow coal pit. During those first few months, Mr. Cairns doubted the wisdom of turning a miner into a merchant. But the business grew, and soon the small shop on

Grace Street, Glasgow, got the family out of debt. Janet, the busy mother of half a dozen, squeezed into her day the keeping of the store. This left Robert free to act as outside salesman of his wares. They prospered.

Then, in the unchanging pattern of a contrary world, a heavy cross dropped on Glasgow's poor. The miners went out on strike. The mine owners, fattened by years of exorbitant profit and slender pay rolls, could afford the work stoppage infinitely more than the workers could. Quickly the cupboards of the city's mining families went bare. The working men, stubborn in their fight for justice, were in agony for their hungry children. In the common bond of the poor, those who had little helped those who had nothing. Grocers, butchers, bakers, and even clothiers, gave credit to the strikers. But no settlement of the strike was in sight. Merchants, unable to raise cash, could not replenish their dwindling stocks.

A ballad, something about the rich growing richer and the poor becoming poorer, was spat from angry throats, in clipped burr, up and down the back streets and alleys of Glasgow.

The Cairns' family and their dry-goods shop were swallowed up in the tide. Refusing no one, and with no income to offset the growing losses, they saw the store on Grace Street become shelf bare and then bankrupt.

It was one thing for the little Scottish mother to whisper words of encouragement to her desperate husband; quite another to choke back the terror that rose in her own heart as she put her hungry children to bed night after night. Perhaps Janet Cairns' very agony drove her into the arms of God. Whatever the secret workings of grace, it was during those black days of want and anxiety that she embraced the Catholic Faith and was baptized in her husband's—and then her own—parish church.

It seemed that the efficacy of the sacrament gave this wife and mother even physical and visible signs of grace. She became the pillar of hope to her despairing partner. She buoyed up her children and seemed to soothe their cranky days of want. She prayed and she planned. Then she convinced her husband that their only chance was for him to follow the scores of desperate miners who were sailing to the New World. So Mr. Cairns sold what he could of their meager possessions, borrowed additional money, and plunged everything on a passage to Boston.

That was in 1885, a year after Sandy's birth. It was a frightful day for all of them when the husband and father sailed out of Glasgow Harbor into the unknown, leaving his penniless wife and six small children to live only on the hope of his success. But in the mining neighborhood where destitution stalked the weary people, this little Catholic mother somehow fed and sheltered her brood through the frantic months of separation.

Meanwhile, on the other side of the Atlantic, Robert Cairns had hurried from Boston to Worcester, Massachusetts, where Scottish friends from home had given him the promise of work. And work he found, and work he did—feverishly. He was racing time. He must call his family to America as soon as possible. First with the city as a laborer, then as melter in a Worcester foundry, he saved enough of his wages in six exhausting months to send passage money to Janet for herself and the children.

Sandy, but eleven months old at the time of sailing, borrowed the memory of his older brothers and sisters to scribble in a letter some forty years later the panic and hilarity of their arrival at Boston.

"We had a two-hour wait, in the rain, at the Boston Station. Father was late meeting us. Mother was worried. We children huddled around her with all our peculiar-looking bundles and grotesque clothes. Then James wandered off to inspect a railroad station 'made in America.' You can imagine what excitement and fun the traveling public were afforded when Mother, missing her dear little boy, cried out at the top of her voice, 'Haw, Jimsey!' "

The family went on to Worcester. There they rented a flat in a three-family house and settled down in St. John's Parish. Sandy was the seventh child of Robert and Janet Cairns—the last one to be born in Scotland. And he was proud of this. He never tired of teasing the four younger children as "wee, bonnie Yankees."

We get glimpses of the family life, in those early years, that reveal the little Scot to be a real Yankee Doodle Dandy. Even at five, Sandy's rollicking, good nature peeked out at the world through laughing eyes. One day the little imp snatched an old biretta, stuck a pair of glasses on his nose, and paraded up and down in front of the parish priest's house. When the old Irish pastor spotted him he roared with delight and dubbed the little tike "Father Foley."

"Father Foley" started school when he was six. This opened up a whole new world to him, for he loved crowds and noise. Though he was quick at verbs and numbers, he is remembered by his school chums for his tricks and pranks and mischief.

The gravest, yet most revealing, crisis of his grammar school days was his eagerness to be an altar boy at St. John's. He made the "team" but lacked the price of his "uniform." Mr. and Mrs. Cairns pinched out a happy life for their children, but there was never any surplus in the family treasury. There certainly was no money for Sandy's cassock and surplice.

This blow staggered the boy. However, he bounced up so

quickly that his relieved parents detected for the first time a selfless spirit in their son, which was to make him a "happy warrior" all the days of his life. His joy and vitality were contagious. Even at the age of ten, Sandy Cairns was the leader of every riot at home, in school, and in the play lots of the neighborhood.

Sandy had a streak of the Scot thriftiness, but a heart as big and open as a mine pit in the Glasgow of his birth. He sold newspapers, ran errands, and clerked in a neighborhood sweet shop. All his earnings he proudly slipped into his mother's apron pocket during the quiet of the evening family Rosary.

Throughout those years, there slowly burned inside the boy a restlessness and groping that he himself did not understand. He knew only that he wanted more than anything else to go to Worcester's Holy Cross College. But something happened at the end of his first year in high school that turned Sandy's dreams for the future into a nightmare of anguish.

He left school, without permission, a few weeks before the end of the term. His plan was to secure a summer job before the rush and competition of his schoolmates would begin. The plan worked. He found a place for himself in the Wesson shoe factory and made "piles" of money that July and August. When September and school time came round again he fell into the meshes of his spring truancy.

Mr. Cairns was a man who frowned on nonsense in the government of his family. "Son," he said, "you left school without asking me; so now you must stay at work."

A storm broke in Sandy's heart, and he was overwhelmed by the cruelty of the fate that he had unwittingly brought on himself.

"I did not realize," he wrote years later, "until that time how deeply set was my resolution to go to Holy Cross; but besides that strong desire, which I mentioned to Father, there was lurking in my mind the unexpressed wish that I might some day become a priest. I cried at my disappointment. My sisters and brothers interceded. Mother spoke to the pastor and the Xaverian Brothers. But my father's Scotch stubbornness prevailed and I went to work. The Brothers told Mother that it was probably God's will that I should not be a priest, but that I should be of greater service to Him in the world. I was convinced by this, and went to work with a will—determined to succeed."

Sandy worked at the Wesson shoe factory for another year. He switched to a job in a machine shop in the city for a while; but disliking that, he tried for and won a job with the Union Laundry. The lad took his place in the working world with seriousness and determination. He enrolled in Worcester Evening High School, to master bookkeeping. As in everything else, Sandy's success at the laundry was won by his ever-contagious good fellowship as much as by his growing commercial ability. He took an International Correspondence School course in advertising, to qualify as sales manager of the company. He planned and formed the Laundry Workers' Union of Worcester—of which he became secretary. In eighteen short but busy months, Sandy saved sufficient money to go in business for himself. He bought out the overall department of the Union Laundry, and developed his venture successfully.

It must not be supposed that the young businessman made a fetish of his work. On the contrary, while he squeezed every bit of his Scottish sagacity into his business enterprise, he found time to throw himself splashingly into the social life of Worcester. A born mimic, a great storyteller, and talented in Scottish step-dancing, Sandy was the spark in every crowd and lit great fires of merriment at the parish socials, minstrel shows, and amateur nights.

It was during these years after his father's "school ruling" that Sandy fell in love with the girl downstairs. Marion Brown's family lived in the same three-decker house. This "bonnie wee lassie," as he called her, won his heart completely, and he courted her for three happy years.

Marion's staunch Protestant convictions, as much as Sandy's loyalty to the Church, led the young couple to the parish priest for counsel. Had the "bonnie wee lassie" faltered in her resolve to bring up her future children in the religion she cherished, then Sandy's future glorious memories would never have been born. But all of Sandy's affectionate pleadings with the girl he loved would not budge the rock of her determination. Sadly, with the wrenching of two great hearts, Sandy gave up his Marion, and Marion her Sandy. Loyalty had conquered human love.

What are the secrets of a heart that bleeds at love's death, but lives on through death to love again? Two whisperings tug against each other. Bitterness at loyalty's reason, against dedication to the reason of loyalty. The victory cry of dedication in the well of Sandy's soul rose to such a crescendo that the painful moan of the bitterness was muffled forever.

Enrolling in new courses at night school, spending long hours planning improvements for his laundry, joining the Adams Debating Society of Worcester, organizing the Evening High School Alumni Association—all these interests and activities tended to heal the heart of a youth who had lost his sweetheart. But they also turned Sandy in on himself, as much as that exploding extrovert could be so turned. His old restlessness was revived.

His feelings confused him. He was stumbling along searching, yet not searching, for a treasure that he was almost afraid to find. He told himself he should be happy.

After all, wasn't he a success? Hadn't he his family to fill his heart? And what of the thousands of friends scattered through all the streets of Worcester, standing like sentries to protect him from this enemy of gnawing loneliness?

Monotonous, even empty, years heeled upon other years of wearier monotony and greater emptiness. It was six years since he had left school. He was twenty-three years old. He knew the sweat of hard labor, the thrill of a colleen close, the roar of a happy audience, the grief for his father's death. But he had never felt the sting and cut and crucifying determination of a man burnt out of himself with the living, flaming fire of thirst for souls. Souls saved by the Redeemer on the hill of Calvary, yet groping still, on barren mountains, for a savior.

Slowly and painfully, Sandy came to realize that this hollowness he felt in his very being could be filled only by some tremendous undertaking—some enormous task that would challenge and absorb his head, his heart, and all his life. Yet he unconsciously shied away from the fire he knew would burn and brand him. He was driven on by eagerness, but time after time braked himself at the brink of realization. He told himself that he was too old, too settled, to be dreaming like a child. He must get hold of himself and exhaust his restlessness in harder work and longer play. Fiercely, he held on to what he had, and beat his thoughts into the familiar groove he knew to be safe and sure and sufficient.

But finally, on a night not unlike many others, when he loitered after class at Evening High to swap stories and ball scores with his friends, a shot was fired that blasted off the chains binding him to the rock of little loves and safe security. The shot was triggered by a chance remark of young Mike Lahey, a classmate. Mike was telling Sandy of his plans to enter Holy Cross College, to go on to the seminary, and to become a priest. Sandy, accustomed to the confidences of younger schoolmates, nodded interest and mumbled words of encouragement.

Then, as if God had truly crammed the hopes and fears of all the years into three little words, Mike asked the inspired question, "How about you?"

The dream, the dare, the dedication, he had fought against overpowered Sandy at last. His mind leaped and jumped and crashed into the middle of a hundred plans that were his answer to Mike's and God's question, "How about you?" He would be a priest. He must be a priest! There was no doubting, no delaying longer. He would be a priest. He hugged the thought till the very warmth of it melted away every obstacle. He would be a priest. He, Sandy Cairns, a priest!

He sold the laundry to his brother Jim. He resigned from his Union job. He bowed out of the dozen clubs and societies that had seemed to make his life so full. He whispered his hopes to his mother. He confided them to his parish priest. And then he raced up the steps of Holy Cross College, to a new life and an old dream—to an eternal challenge. Although he was six years away from textbooks, Sandy plodded and plowed through the studies of high school and college, and he was completely happy.

Holy Cross was the runway for the big takeoff—his approach to the sanctuary. No problem seemed big. No work was too much, to prepare for and insure the goal he had set for himself. He made those days full with half a hundred projects—the school paper, the orchestra, the debating club. He threw himself into everything at college, with the enthusiasm and drive of a man who knew where he was going and wanted nothing else but to get there.

. . . to the altar

Saint Pius X was gloriously reigning in the Chair of Peter. War threatened in Europe. Woodrow Wilson was in the White House. Jack Johnson wore the heavyweight boxing crown of the world. The Boston Braves swept the World Series in four straight. Old Rosebud won the Kentucky Derby. And Robert John Cairns graduated from Holy Cross College.

The year was 1914. On a warm June night, Sandy climbed the back stairs on Dix Street, marched into the kitchen, and laid his diploma in his mother's lap. Everything he had done and said and thought for the past seven years was for this day. And he knew his mother would rejoice with him. The first and longest run in his race to the priesthood was finished. He was ready for the seminary. The altar was in sight. He could now begin to count his spiritual sheep.

Sandy, during his last year at Holy Cross, had volunteered for the mission diocese of Los Angeles-Monterey. His choice was prompted by two considerations. First, he dreamed of spending his priesthood in some faraway place, in poverty and holiness, to save the most abandoned. Secondly, there was the happy coincidence that his former parish priest at Sacred Heart Church in Worcester had been made bishop of that California territory. Sandy was accepted by Bishop Conaty as a candidate, and immediately he began to fall in love with the flock he had not yet seen, but to which God seemed to be calling him.

In the September following graduation, Sandy entered St. Mary's Seminary, Baltimore, to begin the years of prayer and study in preparation for his dreamed-of apostolate among the poor, along California's El Camino Real.

A seminarian's day-in and day-out life in old St. Mary's, as in all seminaries of the Catholic world, had many divisions within itself. This must be so, by the very nature of the training that strives to mold a man in grace and knowledge and judgement according to the full stature of Christ—into the likeness of the One whom he is to imitate. The chapel, the lecture hall, and the ball field are the wells into which the future priest must daily dip deeply if he would fill his heart and life with the reckless kind of love that drove Christ to Calvary for the salvation of the world. Sandy Cairns, six or eight years older than most of his classmates, entered into this serious business with a depth of earnestness and determination that belied his constant surface sparkle.

Yet, it was during those first months in Baltimore, when it could be supposed that he would be swept along in the thrill of his new life, that Sandy suffered most from the pull and drag of impulses he had thought were dead. His trouble was not mainly homesickness but fears inspired by a life yet unknown. In the dark of long nights on his iron cot, the new seminarian grappled with the old doubts of his worthiness for what he was hoping to do with his life. The high ideals set before him by his seminary professors frightened him. Such purity, understanding, and detachment are demanded of a priest! He looked within himself, with strictness and humility, and found only void and barrenness there. To give up? To go on? He was torn between the two.

It is one of the paradoxes of life that what terrifies a man can be routed by a new and greater fear. And that is how, in a way, it was with Sandy. His many worries, and the fear of faltering in the fight to win the lifelong battle of priestly and complete surrender, were conquered by the challenge of an even greater immolation, by a war that knew no talk of truce—much less of surrender.

In the spring of that first year at St. Mary's, Bishop Conaty died, and with him part of Sandy's dream. The part that reached out across the miles to far-off California. But in compensation, something new was born. There was a Patrick J. Byrne, from Washington, studying at the Sulpician seminary. He was one year ahead of Sandy. As once the off-hand query of young Mike Lahey had been the means of grace to light a fire, so the example of the older seminarian enkindled it anew. Shortly after ordination, the young Father Byrne joined the Maryknoll Society.

Maryknoll! The foreign missions! The pagan world! The multitude of souls that must be saved. The seed that must be sown—the harvest to be reaped—in all the despairing, heathen corners of the globe! Yet despite his burning desire, Sandy hardly dared to believe that he heard the whisper of the call once heard by Peter, Paul, and Xavier, before him.

"Come, follow me . . . I will make you to be fishers of men . . . as the Father has sent Me, I also send you . . . to preach the Gospel to the poor . . . to save that which is lost . . . for these also must I bring . . . to speak with new tongues . . . into the whole world . . . and when they persecute you . . . let not your heart be troubled . . . for I have chosen you . . . and I will be with you all days."

Freed, by Bishop Conaty's death, from any obligation to Los Angeles-Monterey, Sandy planned to follow Pat Byrne to the American Foreign Mission Seminary as soon as possible. Back in the days of Worcester, of Glasgow, back into eternity, God had set His heart on this boy's becoming an apostle. During his next vacation from St. Mary's, Sandy went to the Maryknoll headquarters in New York, to apply for admission into that apostolic company, banded together but five years earlier to begin to answer America's call to the foreign missions.

The Catholic Foreign Mission Society of America, later known as Maryknoll, came into being in 1911 when the zeal of two great American priests overflowed the shores of their own country and poured out to all the world. James Anthony Walsh and Thomas Frederick Price met for the first time in 1910, at the Eucharistic Congress in Montreal. It was fitting that on a pilgrimage to a foreign country those two mission-minded men should come together. And each, in his own way, already was a missionary.

Father Walsh, in Boston, was the archdiocesan director of the Society for the Propagation of the Faith. Across his desk flowed an unending stream of appeals from missioners on all the continents—appeals for prayer, and help, and more laborers. Young Father Walsh's heart longed with a great yearning to identify himself with the apostles in the far-off outposts of Asia, Africa, and other mission lands. He often dreamed of himself carrying the Faith to some of the pagan millions who had never heard the redeeming name of Jesus Christ. He became so completely absorbed in the missionary endeavor of the Church that, as Christ Himself once wept over Jerusalem, so did Father Walsh grieve over the billion pagans lying like sheep without a shepherd— orphaned souls born to live and die without the food or raiment of the one true Faith.

There was the urgency of unrequited love in James Anthony Walsh's thirst for souls—a kind of communication of his spirit that excited all who knew or even met him. Thomas Frederick Price fell under this spell that day in Canada. His, too, was an apostolic heart consumed with compassion for half a world not yet knowing the humility of God at Bethlehem or the violence of His love on Calvary.

Father Price had already spent twenty-two years in the priesthood in the backwoods mission area of North Carolina. He was a man who knew war and did not hesitate to lay his victories on the line in new and greater combat.

So it was that two such men met to set such a fire that the heat of it has burned a path around the world and back again. For three years the two planned and prayed in their separate ways, yet knew what they must do together. They presented their plan for a foreign mission society to the American Hierarchy, and with that approval of the bishops of the United States went on to Rome for final Papal blessing.

In September of 1911, on a small plot of land thirty miles up the Hudson from New York City, Father Walsh and Father Price knelt to pray in a rundown farmhouse that came to be the cradle of the giant that now is Maryknoll.

The little band of missioners swelled to seven in a year, and moved from their rented home in Hawthorne to the permanent headquarters of their Society on a high hill overlooking the Hudson River. It was to this knoll dedicated to Mary—Maryknoll—that Sandy Cairns followed Pat Byrne from St. Mary's, Baltimore, in the summer of 1916.

Sandy was "home" at last. At Maryknoll. And yet not really home, for this was but a station, too, along the way to his own land and his own people—across the world, in pagan Asia.

Father Walsh and Father Price ruled with patient love and coaxed out with daring challenge all the hidden drive and courage of the young men who came to them to become apostles.

The eyes of China and all the Far East were upon this newly drafted, apostolic combat team. Souls of Oriental millions called to them. In Rome, the Sacred Congregation of Propaganda Fide, which directs the men and material of the Church's beachheads in mission lands, assigned a territory in South China to the new Society. Now Cairns, and Byrne, and the quickly growing numbers on Mary's hill by the Hudson had a destination for their dreams.

Sandy, when he arrived at New York that September, had already finished two years of theological studies, and had but two more till ordination. At Maryknoll, however, there was more to learn than liturgy and Latin. How do you set a broken bone? What is Confucianism? What kind of fertilizer is best for rice? Where is Kongmoon? When is river water safe for drinking? What's this plumbing all about? The answers to these questions, also, a man must store in his mind against the duties of the days to come.

Together with his classmates at Maryknoll, Sandy devoured every paper, book, and piece of print about China and her millions, to bring closer the new mission field and the day when they would sail for it. Back in Worcester, the Cairns family waited eagerly for the great day of Sandy's ordination.

Another missioner in another day had penned the lines that now raced through the head of Sandy as he thought of his little Scottish mother who had guided and encouraged him through the years to this, the eve of his standing at the altar.

> "You must smile, I know,
>   At what I gave you long ago;
>   Mother, you recall
>   When I was small,
>   The milk-white 'lucky' stone
>   I found and carried home—
>   And the bottled bumblebee
>   I brought for you to see.
>   And you never gave a sign
>   That your delight was less than mine
>   The day I brought into the house
>   A bright-eyed, woolly mouse!
>   When at school I won for you
>   A dozen marbles—oh, so blue;
>   I stole roses from some yard,
>   And in church, a 'holy card.'
>   Now I think of you at night
>   And in the morning when I pray.
>   Accept these sincere lines
>   Of this poor verse of mine;
>   Those former things were worthless
>   And these are oh, so small!
>   But the future still holds all.
>   If our God is kind,
>   In the future I shall find
>   That which brightest beams
>   Among my boyhood dreams—
>   When vested in the priestly white,
>   Underneath the altar light,
>   I can give our God to you!"

The eagerness and the floating feeling that swept Sandy along during the days that brought him closer and closer to his goal, were anchored in cold, hard, fighting reality. The dreams of night are paid for in the harsh, bright light of wary day. At his books, or on his knees, or out roaring on the handball court, Sandy did not balk at the struggle for the holiness he knew a man must have who dared to be "another Christ."

> "To give and not to count the cost;
>   to fight and not to heed the wounds;
>   to labor and not to seek reward,
>   save knowing only that I do Thy holy will, O God."

The lives of all the great missioners of the ages seemed to boil down to the living of this, his favorite prayer. He read of all those heroes who had left everything and had gone out to the frozen wastes of the Arctic, to the steaming jungles of the tropics, to plant the cross of Christ. They were soldiers of Christ, were what he had to be—brave. Not afraid to fight and suffer. Kind and gracious men, who made their homes the houses of the poor. Spending themselves to the last exhausted bit of strength. Healing, teaching, loving the empty lives of those bogged down in pagan hopelessness. Bringing faith and hope and charity to those in destitution and despair.

"I thirst for souls" . . . "other sheep I have" . . . "I, if I be lifted up, will draw all to Myself" . . . "Who shall separate us from the love of Christ?" . . . "forgetting the things that are behind, and stretching forth myself to those that are before . . . to suffer the loss of all things, and count them as dung" . . . "with no one to preach to them, how will they know?" . . . "to go into the whole world and make disciples of all men" . . . "for greater love than this no man hath, that a man lay down his life for his friends" . . . "to preach Christ, and Him crucified . . ."

This was the challenge of Jesus Christ to Robert John Cairns. And he took it. He spent the rest of his life living it.

In the first week of May, 1918, Sandy began his ordination retreat. Perhaps only another priest can know the feeling of unworthiness that crushed Sandy when the time of ordination had come—only another who also has raised his hands for Consecration can understand the fierceness of Sandy's resolution to labor and suffer and pray and console, and empty himself, all the days of his priesthood, for the salvation of souls.

On May 18, Sandy knelt in the sanctuary of the New York archdiocesan seminary chapel, at Dunwoodie, at the feet of Cardinal Farley. This was the time! This was the day! This was the very moment of triumph. A kind of delirium of glory fevered his body. Crashing together in his head and heart were joy and pride and zeal and victory. Trickles of nervous perspiration ran down his back under the stiff, new vestments. The hot flush of excitement burned scarlet on his freckled cheeks.

The Cardinal prayed on, in the reverent whispers of the Sacred Rite. The divine words of consecration, challenge, and commission exploded in Sandy's ears. "Imitate what you handle . . . whose sins you shall forgive, they are forgiven . . . thou art a priest forever . . ."

Thunder roared. Lightning struck. The sun burst. The heavens opened inside of Sandy. This was the priesthood. This was his. This was the eternal moment of his consecration, of his becoming another Christ—a priest. He was "Father" Sandy. Father Robert J. Cairns.

His mother and his brothers and sisters had, of course, come from home for his ordination. He celebrated his first Mass at Maryknoll, for the family, the next morning; and then together all returned to Worcester. On the Sunday following, at St. Paul's—the family's parish church—Father

Sandy sang his first Solemn Mass. That morning no one could count the throng that knelt in adoration around a little Scottish mother in her glory as her son, their own Sandy, bent and said the words, and brought down God from Heaven. This boy belonged to Worcester. This priest was their own. And yet they knew he would soon leave them to travel off to fabled China to bring to other mothers' sons, to far-off cities of the East, a day like this that now was theirs in Worcester. They knew he'd go, and they were proud and happy in their loss.

Father Sandy spent the next few weeks at home, with his family, in the old "three-decker" on Dix Street. Each morning the neighbors saw him walk the two blocks to St. Paul's Church, with his mother, for Mass. These days were such a time of joy for Janet Cairns, as she watched her son at the altar, that she must have smiled and nodded in her prayers, for the realization that all the little hurts and crosses through the years of her family's growing up should merit such a great reward as this from the good God.

The vacation days sped by in a round of happy visiting Old friends from Evening High School, the boys of the Laundry Workers' Union, his priest-professors at Holy Cross College—he got around to them all. The stiff Roman collar of his new priesthood never for a moment cramped the bouncy good humor that made him welcome and remembered everywhere. And Father Sandy burned into his heart the memory of the faces of these friends, the old familiar haunts of his youth, the worn back steps to his mother's kitchen, the dark and quiet sacristy of St. Paul's, and all the other things that would be his to cherish in his days in China, half a world away from Worcester.

He returned to Maryknoll, in time to wish an envious "God speed" to the first Maryknoll priests to leave for the Orient, and "home." How he had longed and prayed, and

promised things to God, that he might have been among
those to lead the way. But Father Walsh had other work for
him at home. He had still to wait before he'd hear the victory chant of Maryknoll's Departure Hymn . . .

"Go forth, apostles of God's tender mercies,
  To tell to men the tidings of great joy.
  Like angels, speak ye words of faith and hope undying.
      Farewell, brothers, farewell.

How beautiful the feet of God's apostles,
  In holy exile, led to fields afar,
  To teach men of God's love—brave troubadours of Christ.
      Farewell, brothers, farewell.

Go forth, farewell for life, O dearest brothers;
  Proclaim afar the sweetest name of God.
  We meet again one day in heaven's land of blessings.
      Farewell, brothers, farewell."

Father Sandy was assigned to travel up and down the
country giving vocation talks, getting help, and increasing
interest in the foreign missionary cause, among the Catholics of America. Newark, Philadelphia, Chicago—everywhere he went he won support and staunch friends for
Maryknoll. There are priests and Sisters, from New York
and Seattle and Boston, in the fields afar today, who can
hearken back to Father Cairns' words that stirred and
urged them on to go abroad and fight for Christ.

Another of his duties in those months after ordination
was the week-end help he gave in preaching and hearing
confessions, in some parishes neighboring Maryknoll. This
work Father Sandy especially loved. It was a taste, and in a
way a test, of all he'd do when he got "home" to China.
The yearning to be off, remained strong in him. He felt the

very real pull of other sheep that must be his—twelve thousand miles away. Father Cairns was a man who had learned to wait—for Holy Cross, for ordination, and finally for China—but in his waiting he was never idle. More time to learn to love, to sacrifice, to get a thirst for souls, which would make this stocky Scot a real priest to every man he should meet until his martyrdom.

. . . on to China

Father Sandy was on the West Coast, in the spring of 1920, making the rounds, building up Maryknoll's family of supporters. His base was San Francisco, but he traveled up and down the coast telling Catholics everywhere of men like the martyred-missioner Theophane Venard, and of teeming pagan Asian cities, of a half-billion Chinese souls who needed hope and love and Christ; telling all whom he met how they were needed in the cause, how they themselves could help.

Then it arrived. He received the word in Seattle. The news came on April 7—marching orders from Maryknoll. "To China." Father Sandy finally had won.

Although he continued his mission promotion work up to the very eve of his departure, Father Sandy was busy the next five months getting ready—packing, bidding farewells, arranging passport and visas, making passage reservations, and clearing up the other odds and ends a person must do before emigrating to a foreign land.

Father Sandy saw himself as a true emigrant, and not merely as one going abroad to do a work or carry out a mission. His was a journey to the place that held all his hopes in life, for love and labor. To China . . . To his "new world," the one that lay westward and westward until it was East. To his own land and people of adoption. To new, yet age-old customs he must learn, and to dialects he must master—the names of which he could not yet remember or pronounce.

Father Sandy made a flying trip to Worcester for good-byes to his mother and brothers and sisters, all of whom seemed reluctant, yet anxious, to see him go. Then on to New York, to join the other five missioners who made up Maryknoll's third departure group.

It was on September 25, twenty-eight months after his ordination, that Father Sandy set sail from San Francisco. The other Maryknollers with him on the trip were men he had grown to love and to depend on as his brothers. There was Father Tony Hodgins, from Brooklyn; newly ordained Joseph Donovan, whose home in Pittsburgh came to see two other brothers follow in the footsteps of this family leader; Boston's Father George Wiseman; Father Bill McKenna from Baltimore; and Father Frederick Dietz of Oberlin, Ohio.

From San Francisco Bay their ship, traveling the northern sea route across the Pacific, made no stop until it reached the port of Yokohama, on the main island of the Japanese group. It was the young priests' first glimpse of the Orient. They were not "home" yet, but they were in the neighborhood.

The group had a one-day stopover at this first port of call. The missioners spent the time visiting Tokyo, an hour's run by rail from the port city. Father Dietz, in a diary he kept of the voyage and which he later sent back to

Maryknoll, recalled the glorious history of the early Church in that island empire. This was the land where persecution could not kill the Faith, the place where thousands of Catholic families, tenaciously and heroically, clung to their religion through two and a half long, dark centuries without clergy or the Holy Sacrifice. The record of their sufferings was the eternal pride of the Church and the wonder of a marveling world.

Japan had been left without a single priest after a bloody persecution at the turn of the 17th century. The Church went underground, and lived once again in hiding as it did in the Roman days of the catacombs. The people lived on faith and hope and loyalty, and died in martyrdom. Six generations of Japanese remained firm, anxiously waiting a time of peace, when priests could once more shepherd them. When the day of toleration for the Church did come, and missioners reached the shores of Japan, the foreign priests could hardly bring themselves to believe the situation they encountered.

This weary, priestless flock—whose heritage was blood—was wary in giving quick welcome. The Japanese, who had remained faithful to the Church through generations, had three questions to ask, three marks of orthodoxy to be assured of in the new arrivals, before they gave allegiance to them. Their treasure, handed down through years of precious guarding, must not be lost. In the little new church in Nagasaki on St. Patrick's Day in 1865 they asked of the priests:

"Do you have a leader who sits in Peter's chair in Rome?"
"Do your ministers of Sacrifice and Sacrament observe the priestly rule of celibacy?"
"Do you love and honor her who, in virginity, bore the Son of God?"

These were the solemn queries made by an anxious people; and only when the priests identified themselves with the true Church, did the faithful descendants of Japan's first Catholics kneel in joy and gratitude.

The Maryknollers during their short visit in Japan visited Tokyo's largest Catholic school, and were guests of honor at a banquet given there by the Brothers of Mary. But there was a story to that, and Father Sandy was in the middle of it.

It happened that when the travelers arrived in the capital city, although the Brothers were expecting them, there was no one at the station to meet the newly arrived missioners. The priests made several attempts to get across to the shouting, laughing crowd which quickly gathered around them in the train depot that they wanted directions to the Morning Star Catholic School somewhere in the city. The effort was in vain and the missioners were about to give it up as a hopeless job. A nodding, bowing, smiling pedicab driver, in a last attempt to be helpful, tried to force them on to a train southbound for Osaka. Then Father Sandy got his inspiration. He pushed and elbowed his way, with the five other priests running interference, through all the noise and crush to a telephone he spotted over at the other end of the station. "Hello, hello," he roared into the mouthpiece, above the din of the ever-growing mob which seemed intent on seeing this thing through to the end. "Hello, hello," he yelled again. And then the answer came—a fast, loud blast of angry Japanese. It gradually dawned on Father Sandy that his "hello" could mean no more than a dog's bark to the Japanese operator. Father Sandy howled with delight at this development.

Hours and circling miles later when the lost brigade reached the big brick school, the worried Brothers opened their doors and hearts and banquet hall to a happy, weary, laughing band of Padres.

Early the next morning, the *S.S. Nanking* with all aboard shoved off and sailed south with the tide toward Shanghai. It passed hundreds of patch-sailed fishing junks in the choppy, muddy waters of the Yellow Sea that day, and the missioners knew that they were near their land—their China.

As soon as the ship had tied up in berth on the Shanghai Bund, Father Sandy and his companions fell over one another in their rush to touch their feet to Chinese soil. These men were travelers no longer, nor were they exiles in any sense that men have come to use that word. The priests, with all the complex thoughts and feelings and impressions that piled up inside of them, could not confuse the single, thrilling fact that they were home.

How can memories be sorted when they flood in upon a man with the speed of sixty jumping seconds every minute; when they are made up of all the color, dash, and clamor that is a Chinese city? At that moment each peddlar's yell, each ragged youngster's whoop, every flaming colored sign and fascinating shop, the darting bike-cabs, the shuffling bulk of water buffaloes hauling carts, old men smoking in the sun, a young girl hanging wash on jutting bamboo poles, a baby falling, crying in the street—all, all these things were quickly forged and riveted in Father Sandy's head and heart until they were a part of him.

The Maryknollers spent two full days in Shanghai. In their eager attempt to see as much of the city as possible they leaped in desperate haste from place to place, from sight to sight. They visited Zicawei, the Catholic quarter, and knelt, with tired coolies, prosperous-looking merchants, mothers nursing infants, pushing and giggling school children, for afternoon Benediction at St. Ignatius Church. They stopped off at hospitals and clinics around the city, too, meeting groups of missionary Sisters from Ireland, Italy, France, and Spain. The tyro missioners made a one-night stand, in their barnstorming, at St. Joseph's Hospice. There they were welcomed and feted by "St. Joseph's Coolie"— the saintly Lo Pa Hong, who with his great wealth, all of his time, and his reckless charity, had built a Catholic center to nurse and care for Shanghai's sick and poor. Cripples and fugitives and unwed mothers and the aged and orphans had in this man a father. All were welcome there, and no one was ever turned away. It was with great joy that this apostolic Catholic layman entertained the Maryknollers whom he hoped and prayed were the vanguard of a huge army of missioners that would come from America to lead his people into the Faith.

The next morning the priests were off on the last leg of their voyage, to Hong Kong. As their ship traveled south along the coast, Father Sandy spent many hours on deck looking toward the mainland, thinking of all the things he had already seen and planning all the things that he would do in the future. His mind went back to all that he had read of the Church's struggle through the centuries to plant the Faith in China. It was the story of brave apostles, bitter persecution, and many martyrs. He was part of it all now, and he was proud and happy. Perhaps God would even ask him to lay down his life for the Faith, as St. Thomas the Apostle did in the first century when he traveled, as tradition says, to fabled Cathay to bring the Gospel to the Emperor and people of this kingdom. Or perhaps like the missioners who followed Thomas—the Dominicans, Franciscans, and Jesuits who planted the truth, then watered the seed with their blood to bring a harvest of Chinese souls to God. Father Sandy recalled with apostolic envy the labors of the Italian Jesuit Ricci who, in the 17th century, by his great wisdom and holiness won the heart of the Emperor and a high place in the court of Peking, and blazed a trail for all future missioners to follow. He thought also of the martyrs of the Boxer Rebellion—those scores of Chinese men, women, and children who in his own time joyfully went to death rather than deny Christ and the Cross. Father Sandy dared to hope that God would give him, also, the grace of martyrdom, that his blood might become the seed of many Chinese conversions.

On a hot Sunday afternoon in late October, five weeks after they had sailed under the Golden Gate Bridge and out into the Pacific, the men of Maryknoll's third departure group reached Hong Kong. The *Nanking,* however, did not tie up at the dock, but transferred all disembarking passengers and baggage to sampans to be shuttled ashore. The six missioners gingerly lowered themselves into the tiny, narrow, bobbing boats—whose very name in Chinese, "three planks," tells everything about them. As Father Sandy and the others neared the wharf they spotted a group of white-robed figures waving. Closer, closer, the loaded sampans inched their way through the choppy waters of the harbor until the passengers could make out the men in white. They shouted, yelled, and waved in excitement. These were the Maryknoll veterans who had preceded them out from America.

There on the pier were the pioneers of the first departure group, Father Walsh, Father Ford, and Father Meyer. Father Price, co-founder of the new Society, who had led the vanguard into the fight, fell in battle eleven months after the band arrived in the Orient. He was caught up-country with appendicitis, and by the time he could get to Hong Kong and a hospital it was too late to save his life. He died and was buried in a lonely foreign grave in Hong

Kong's Happy Valley Cemetery. Yet not really lonely or foreign, for he was among his missionary sons and in the land they had all adopted as their own. Years later Father Price's relics were taken to Maryknoll, New York, and laid beside the remains of Bishop James Anthony Walsh, so that the shrines of these two saintly men could be an inspiration to the waves and waves of future missioners that would pour out from Maryknoll to all the world.

Also waiting on the dock as the sampans with the new missioners jockeyed for position to tie up at the wharf, were Father Vogel and Father McShane and Father O'Shea, the three who had arrived in China just twelve months earlier. News of home and news of the new mission field were exchanged by the men in this happy reunion of the Maryknoll family overseas.

Hong Kong, a British Crown Colony, was ceded to England by the Chinese government in 1847, and included not only the rock island itself, but also the strip of coast on the mainland, known as Kowloon. Additional land was later leased from the Chinese, enlarging the colony to an area about one third the size of Rhode Island, jutting into the mainland of South China. Although this whole territory is administered by the British, it is, in culture and way of life, really part of China. The population is 99% Chinese, and everything about the place is completely Oriental.

While the other new arrivals joined the veteran Maryknollers on their return to the mainland and the mission field, Father Sandy was assigned to remain in Hong Kong to act as financial administrator for the men, establish a Procure, and prepare a headquarters for the newly-founded Maryknoll Sisters, a group of whom would soon arrive in the Far East to become partners in the work with the Maryknoll Fathers.

His assignment was not a disappointment to Father

Sandy although he did long to begin actual mission work in the villages of South China. He knew that his assigned job was a vital one. He threw himself with energy and enthusiasm into this work. Meanwhile, he saw to it that he had time to meet and get to know the Chinese, to study Cantonese, and to become familiar with the ways and customs of the people.

Father Sandy needed all his Scot stubbornness, and almost more Christian patience than he possessed, when he tackled the study of the language. There are many theories advanced by teachers as to the best method of learning Cantonese, but Father Sandy came to know that all these reduced themselves to hard, hard work. The dialect of South China is a tonal one, which means that any given Chinese sound takes its meaning from the tone of voice used. There are nine tones that give nine different meanings to the same sound. For example, the English transliteration of the Cantonese word for "tea" is "cha." But tea is "cha" in the seventh tone. "Cha" in the first tone means "fork." In the third, it means "marvelous," and so on through the nine tones. This opens many pits into which a foreigner may fall. Father Sandy did his share of falling. He was fond of telling the predicaments into which his howlers involved him. Once in a Hong Kong coffee shop when asking for a piece of cake Father Sandy, juggling the tones, unwittingly found that his order sent the waiter running to the street for a policeman. Another time he so confused the tones in an attempt to tell his cook not to bother with meat for supper that he had the lad vigorously denying evenings spent in gambling.

Father Sandy, if he became discouraged, never gave up his relentless struggle to master Cantonese. He knew that to tell his flock of the love and mercy of God he must speak their language. His fellow missioners maintained that Father

Sandy, even after twenty years in China, was still a mean mauler of the tones, but they always hastened to add that his genuine love for the people made him infinitely more understood than even he himself realized.

Father Sandy spent nearly two years on the Hong Kong assignment, but that was not overlong to acquaint himself with the customs and thinking of the people and to prepare for active missionary labor. Centuries before, a hero of his —Matteo Ricci—wrote in a diary some of the million and one unchanging things a missioner must know if he is to become identified with the Chinese.

"When a family is receiving at home," Ricci wrote, "the one in charge takes a chair in both hands and places it in the position of honor for the visitor. Then he dusts it off with his hand, though there will be no sign of dust on it at all." He observed of the Chinese that "they do not use forks or spoons or knives for eating, but rather polished sticks, about a palm and a half long, with which they are very adept in lifting any kind of food to their mouths, without touching it with their fingers." Father Ricci goes on: "If any of the children are absent at the time of the death of a parent, the entire ceremony of obsequies is deferred for their return. If a prominent person is absent when his parent dies, he erects a monument where he and his friends visit to pay their respects. After that he returns home and arranges for the funeral. It is a matter of strict law, admitting of no exception, for a son to return on such an occasion, no matter what public office he may hold."

By constantly visiting Chinese homes, chatting for hours on end with the school children, poking into shops and stalls, stopping to talk with ricksha drivers, and even attending Chinese operas, Father Sandy during those days in Hong Kong sought to know the people and to become Chinese in everything. His priestly heart knew that only by meeting the people in their own way of life, only by showing love and respect for their customs and their culture, could he hope to lead them into the one true Church where there is neither American, Italian or Chinese—but all are children of the same Father in Heaven.

Father Sandy delighted in reading the tales and legends of ancient China. He was quick to recognize the value of these to lead the pagan mind from fable across the bridge of truth to the Gospel stories of divine reality.

He found still another way, during those days in Hong Kong, to add to his treasure of mission lore. Hundreds of missioners, from every province of China, were continually coming down to the island colony from their upcountry missions to buy medicines for their dispensaries, books for their schools, for visits to the doctor, perhaps to be fitted for new eyeglasses, or to see a dentist. These men, many of whom had spent twenty, thirty, forty years in China, were badgered by the young Maryknoller until they shared with him their methods and secrets of fruitful mission work. In this way Father Sandy came to know, before his time as it were, the things that veteran apostles had learned only after a lifetime of trial and error. He had the time and the opportunity as he went about his procuration work in Hong Kong to sift and store in his mind all these things for the future. One thing, in particular, Father Sandy became convinced of the more he listened to the experiences of the old China hands—the need of building up a native clergy. Here was the hope for the harvest—Chinese boys who would become shepherds of their own people.

Unfortunately, for the growth of the Church in China there had been a school of thought among some missioners that the Chinese were not yet ready in large numbers to join the ranks of the priesthood. The influence of these men—whose short-sighted policy is made somewhat understandable by an appreciation of the stress placed on priests under constantly recurring persecution—slowed down the progress of conversions over all the country. Ecclesiastically China is divided into prefectures and vicariates. In none of these areas could the foreign missioners alone begin adequately to reach all of the teeming millions entrusted to their care. Over and over, Father Sandy heard this story. The more he listened, the more he was resolved to make the fostering of Chinese vocations a rule of his apostolate.

Father Sandy was not advocating a new crusade. Powerful voices had been raised, in North China, to close the ranks and charge. The leader was Father Vincent Lebbe. Father Anthony Cotta, a wise and holy missioner, who had come out to China half a century before with the French Vincentians, was another tiger in the fight for a native clergy. Burning with zeal for the conversion of this noble race, Father Cotta saw that the only hope, the only answer to the impossibility of a few thousand missioners' preaching to four hundred and fifty million Chinese was the erection of local seminaries to provide an army of co-laborers to work side by side with German, French, Spanish, Irish priests in reaping the great harvest of the most populous nation on earth. He took his plan, born of long years of experience and fervent prayer, to his superiors first, and then to the bishops of China. His final appeal was to the Sacred Congregation of Propaganda Fide in Rome. This last was an impassioned plea to the Cardinal Protector of the Church's world-wide mission fields to encourage and foster a native clergy in China. Father Cotta concluded his report to Rome with the now-famous prayer: "I beg God to let me live to prostrate myself at the feet of a Chinese bishop." Father Cotta subsequently joined Maryknoll and it was there, at the Society's headquarters in New York, that his life-long hope was more than realized—he knelt at the feet of visiting Cardinal Tien and whispered, "Now dost thou dismiss Thy servant, O Lord, in peace."

It was the same spirit, bolstered by the example of Father Cotta's apostolic leadership, that drove Father Sandy to work and pray during all his priestly life for a Chinese clergy.

Life continued for Father Sandy in Hong Kong in the ever-increasing pace he set for himself. Visiting the sick, helping the poor, catechizing children—all these works he performed in addition to his administrative duties for the Maryknollers upcountry. By the fall of 1922 he had completed, in a way, his work in the British colony. He had welcomed and established the Maryknoll Sisters in their first foundation in the Far East. In his solicitude for these American women who had come to be co-workers in the saving of souls, who had left home and country, all, to give their selfless lives to make Christ and His Mother known to a pagan world, Father Sandy became a pillar on which they could lean in those first pioneering days. He was an ever generous and understanding spiritual father to them in their problems.

A short time later Father Sandy received the call he so eagerly awaited, for which he had so intently prepared. Father James E. Walsh, superior of the Maryknoll priests in China, soon to be consecrated vicar apostolic of Kongmoon and the first bishop of Maryknoll, sent word to Father Sandy that he was to come upcountry immediately. With his measure of joy now full Father Sandy at once packed his belongings and sailed up the Pearl River into China—and home!

. . . in the work

It was to Yeungkong Father Cairns was heading—not a hard place to find, but three days and two boat changes from Hong Kong.

On the trip to Yeungkong Father Sandy was the center of attraction. The slow, deliberate stream of Cantonese that flowed from his stammering lips, the blue eyes, the grayish red head, and the strong-looking chunky bulk of him, at first amazed, and then delighted his fellow passengers. They bombarded him with questions.

"Where is the Beautiful Country scholar going?"

"What is the honorable teacher's name?"

"How many sons does the honorable firstborn have?"

"Do all westerners have big noses? and wear leather shoes?"

On deck, perched first on a chicken basket, next on a bale of cotton, Father Sandy spent a happy time laughing and singing and chatting his way to the port city in southern

Kwangtung Province which was to be his first field of battle.

At noon of the third day on the water, Yeungkong came in sight. The low, drab buildings of the city seemed to rise up out of nowhere, just beyond the stretch of rice paddies, and beckon to Father Sandy's creeping junk to hurry. As it squeezed in between half a hundred sampans for a landing, Father Sandy saw his new pastor, Father Ford, light a string of firecrackers and toss them into the air. Above the shouts of the boatmen, "easy," "to the right," "slower, slower," he heard Father Ford roar, "Welcome, Sandy!"

Yeungkong was the first mission parish of the Maryknoll Fathers in China. They had inherited a chapel, living quarters, and 2000 Christians from the French priests who were there before them. By Christmas of 1920 the American priests had already fanned out to towns and markets as far as 300 miles away. Father Ford, alone in Yeungkong, was desperately in need of help.

Father Sandy's arrival doubled the chances for Yeungkong's million and a quarter pagans to hear about the Church, and to see the tenderness and gentleness of Christian charity in action.

Father Sandy, apprentice to Father Ford, had a truly apostolic teacher. This priest from Brooklyn led the way and his student followed. All his life, Francis Xavier Ford was to lead. He blazed the trail in Yeungkong, and a few years later when the Holy See entrusted a new mission territory, Kaying, to Maryknoll, Father Ford pioneered there also. In 1935, he was consecrated bishop, vicar apostolic of the Kaying vicariate. This successor of the Apostles, like St. Paul himself, labored unceasingly to lead forth a holy people approved by God. He established in his see one of the strongest groups of Chinese clergy in all of China, founded a native Sisterhood, and erected Catholic schools in every mission parish. Bishop Ford cared for his flock with a divine jealousy. When the flood of Communist terror and persecution swept down through China after World War II, this good shepherd remained with his sheep. He suffered under Mao Tze-tung, was tortured, died, and was buried. When word of his martyrdom reached the outside world, a Mass of triumph in red, not black vestments, was celebrated to honor his memory and his sacrifice. In the eulogy a brother missionary bishop declared: "Some of the noblest blood that has ever watered this earth since Christ's crucifixion was the martyr's blood of Francis Xavier Ford."

It was in Yeungkong, with this same Father Ford, that Father Sandy began his missionary labors. The seasoned missioner was tireless in his rounds of the city and visits to the clan villages that circled the urban hub like spokes of a wheel. He made contacts everywhere for the Church, interesting the rich and the poor, farmers, officials, and merchants in the sublime and redeeming doctrine of our Holy Faith. By his care and visits to the sick, his help to the poor, his respect for the aged, and his gentleness with the children, he did just what he set out to do; to win the hearts of the people to himself, and through him to Christ.

From Father Ford Father Sandy learned well the methods and techniques best suited to make converts in South China. In a country where the "other sheep" are reckoned in the hundreds of millions, the shepherd must study and plan and calculate how, in the little time given him, he can best bring the greatest number of these "others" into the fold.

First of all, Father Sandy learned, the missioner, on arriving at a pagan town or village, must look around for the peoples' greatest need. It might be for a school, a burial society, improved farming methods, a clinic, an orphanage, or perhaps an artesian well or a hostel for the old and feeble. Whatever be the most pressing need, the missioner must encourage a solution and use it as a fulcrum to lift the people into the Church. Among a people who have been molded and set in the cast of paganism for five thousand years, it is courting almost certain rejection to attempt to plant, in unprepared ground, the tree of the cross of the Crucified. Christ Himself spent three years breaking ground. He gave sight to the blind, cleanness to lepers, the power to walk to the lame, speech to the dumb, and life to the dead. Only then He took the final count of His disciples on the eve of His Passion.

When the missioner has decided on his avenue of approach to win the good will of the people, he must follow that method with infinite patience and unfaltering step. Perhaps it may take months, even years, to kill the suspicion and wariness of the people. One French missioner in Canada's frozen north lived and worked and prayed for fourteen discouraging years among the Eskimos without a single Baptism. But he held on, and today the Church is flourishing in that land of snow and ice.

Father Ford pointed out to his new curate that the pagan heart—ignorant and devoid of pity, mercy, and compassion —is at first confused by Christian charity. It looks for some dark motive for the missioner's selflessness it has not yet discovered. But as inevitable as dripping water making an impression on rock, so does constant love overwhelm the one loved. In the end, once suspicions are removed, love can conquer any human heart.

Once the missioner has won the confidence and affection of his people, it is a short step for him to the point where he can explain the reason for his love and why he left his home to come and live among them in the first place at all. Good people everywhere, especially among the poor, because their very want has schooled them to separate the generous from the greedy, invariably begin to wonder if the missioner's doctrine and religion can bring the same joy and peace and contentment to their lives as they see in his. At this juncture the priest's battle is already half won. He can move in to clinch the final victory for Christ.

Father Sandy watched, and learned, and helped Father Ford in the next phase, in the next move in the missionary strategy to win over souls to the camp of Christ. The opening of a catechumenate requires all the timing, preparation, and coordination of a military invasion. If, for example, a handful of people in a village of fifty or sixty families are anxious to become Catholics, they are encouraged to sign up at least half the population of the village to begin the study of the doctrine with them. This is not an economic move, on the part of the missioner, but an assurance that his converts later will not be dragged back to superstitious practices by the overwhelming numbers of their pagan neighbors. When the leaders of the group desiring to embrace the Faith do swell the ranks to the necessary strength, the priest must discipline and make heavy demands on the neophytes lest some be misled into believing that they are doing the missioner a favor by becoming Catholics, rather than being convinced that they are enriching their own lives with the treasure of the one true religion.

During the four months, the usual time each catechumenate runs in South China, the pastor keeps trained catechists in the village, men for the men and women for the women, to teach the people the prayers and the catechism lessons. Father Ford impressed on Father Cairns the absolute necessity of frequent visits by the missioners to the catechumenate. It is the priest who must resolve difficulties, expound the doctrine, reassure the faltering, in general show the catechumens that he is their spiritual father, prepared and eager to make any sacrifice for them.

Father Ford learned that bringing the people into the Center to live at the mission compound for the final two weeks before baptism went a long way toward creating that ease and familiarity with the sacramentals of the Church which are so necessary for a full Catholic life. These two weeks gave the candidates for baptism an opportunity to recite their morning and night prayers together, attend daily Mass, be present for Rosary and Benediction, and make the Stations of the Cross. Father Sandy quickly saw the advantages of this stratagem of Father Ford and used it himself ever after.

At the end of the four months of study the missioner holds a final examination. The final judgment of worthiness depends as much on the faithful attendance at class during the catechumenate, the effort made in studying the doctrine, and the sincerity of the candidate, as on word for word answers to the catechism questions. Seldom are the very old, plagued as they are with tricky memories, turned away or required to go through a second catechumenate.

Then comes the great day of baptism! This is the goal, and the triumph of the apostle. To give back to God His children; and to give the children their Father and their inheritance to Heaven. To lead the hopeless out of the darkness into the brightness of the Light of the World. To gather up soiled pagan souls and wash them snow-white in the Blood of the Lamb. The baptismal day of his people is the missioner's hope and fulfillment and victory . . . his joy and his crown. The first class to receive the Sacrament after Father Sandy's arrival in Yeungkong was a large one. The memory of the happiness and elation of that day sustained and spurred him on in the years to come, whenever the burden of discouragement began to buckle his knees.

Father Sandy, getting more facility with the language all the time, was giving more and more help to Father Ford in preaching, hearing confessions, and directing the catechumenates. In spite of this—indeed, because of this—Father Walsh, the mission superior at Kongmoon, decided to send Father Sandy to be pastor at Fachow City, a corner of the Maryknoll Vicariate which up until that time had been unattended because of the lack of a shepherd to send to these sheep.

Here was a new and great adventure for Father Sandy. This was the test of a man—to go off into a stronghold of paganism where there had never been a resident priest, to meet the devil on his own ground, to whip him and all his works and pomps, and to come off with the victory. As soon as Father Sandy could find Fachow on the map, plan his route, pack his Mass kit and mission equipment, hire passage on a cargo junk, he was off.

The market town of Fachow hung onto the mainland only by its southern and western arms and seemed to be slipping into the China Sea on one side, and sliding slowly into the Flower River on the other. It was nearly three hundred miles down the coast from Yeungkong, if the extra shore-hugging route of in-and-out detour be added to the distance of the trip. The South China seacoast is a continuous series of coves, inlets, and small bays, that offer shelter to the junk fleets from the sudden and violent storms so frequent there.

In November, 1923, eleven months after his arrival in China, Father Sandy set out on a lopsided, dirty, raggysailed junk for his new mission parish. His "battle-wagon" traveled in a two hundred ship convoy. This was necessary for two reasons. The first and most important one was mutual protection from the pirate fleets that stalked those coastal waters; the other was to have a lifeboat near, in the calculated risk a flimsy 30-foot junk was taking to start out on such a trip in the first place. Father Sandy's voyage from Father Ford's port parish to Fachow took ten days, but the trip was a quiet one, free of storms and unmolested by pirates.

While it was true that Fachow previously never had had a resident priest, a French missioner for seven or eight years before Father Sandy's arrival visited the place two or three times each year on his mission trips from Pakhoi. The French priest paid annual rent for a small shop in the market place. By a long stretch of the imagination it might be said that Fachow had a temporary Catholic Church. It was to this chapel, priest's house and dispensary—all contained in one dark, damp room—that Father Sandy came and moved in bag and baggage.

"The Catholic Chinese gave me a welcome," he wrote in a letter home. "They swept and cleaned, helped us with our baggage, and showed in other ways that they were happy to have a resident priest. The family next door sent over a chicken and some oranges. We like the place, and love the people."

If anyone needed proof of Father Sandy's tremendous good humor, his unbounded optimism, and his downright ruggedness, he had it all here. The fact of the matter was that the one-room hovel he called home was smack in the heart of the noisy marketplace, had no windows but did own a leaky roof, and was ten times too small for his needs. As for the Catholic Chinese who welcomed him to Fachow, the truth was that they numbered exactly—three. Only a man with a great heart, absolutely fearless, could have hung a "Home, Sweet Home" sign over the bamboo door of that shack in Fachow. Father Sandy could, and did.

Where to start? First he must take a census. He soon became a familiar sight as he went from shop to house, to stall, to hut, up and down every lane and alley of the city, in his jolly way poking into every merchant's and coolie's family history. The children romped after him everywhere, and the curious spectators smiled their approval when he would stop, as he often did, at a candy vendor's cart and treated a hundred, two hundred giggling, excited youngsters to a feast of sugared sweet potato cuts.

The town covered, Father Sandy moved out with his census book to the countryside. He found that he had twenty-five clan villages in his parish, scattered like buoys on a fishnet in a sea of rice paddies covering an area the size of Lake Michigan. His final count was three baptized Catholics in Fachow itself, and eighty-three more in his village empire. This was a start, but a pitifully small one, when he placed it against 3,339,504—the Chinese Postal Guide's total population figure for the area. Father Sandy did not for a moment see his vocation to be spiritual father only to the eighty-six; rather his heart and his hopes embraced every single one of the three and a half million men, women, and children in Fachow.

Studying the situation, searching for Fachow's major need as Father Sandy had so well learned to do from Father Ford, he came to the conclusion that a school would be the best tool with which to hammer down the closed door of the city's heart.

"Respect the aged, fuss over the young, and you win all" was an old Chinese proverb that Father Sandy baptized and made into a kind of 9th beatitude in his mission work. A school for Fachow's boys and girls would surely take care of the "fussing over the young" part. He did not delay, either, and a month after his arrival, Holy Cross School was a reality. A fellow missioner who visited Father Sandy the following spring wrote back to Maryknoll, New York, a short but revealing report about the sagacious Scot from Worcester, and about the new Holy Cross.

"The influence of Rome in Fachow consisted entirely of two catechists, a Scotch burr, and energy galore. There was a whirlwind of multifold activities. Chief among them was the school named after Father Cairns' Alma Mater. Holy Cross school functioned in an abandoned temple next door to the Mission. The pagan owners loaned the premises rent-free. That meant that the price of the accommodation really consisted in periodically ejecting soldiers who make a practice of using temples as temporary hotels. The service was performed so often by Father Cairns that he became bored at gazing down the muzzles of German Mausers."

The school was doubly successful from the very beginning—both scholastically for the children and propagandawise for the Church. Soon Holy Cross was running so smoothly under the direction of the catechists that Father Sandy found more and more time to go out into the country on mission trips. That was the work he loved most—the journeys which brought him closest to his people, in their own villages and in their own homes.

There is a long letter still preserved, written by Father Sandy in his inimitable and bouncy style, about the laughs and tears of mission trips in South China.

"In a Chinese village, in the privacy of a bedroom in a public square, with a tiny lamp spitting peanut oil at you, did you ever try to recite your breviary? With ducks and chicks, and cattle and pigs nosing around in the same room with you, did you ever try to shave?"

Further on in the letter he tells of a sick-call to bring the last sacraments to a dying woman. "I reached her mud home late at night. She died a holy death two hours after I anointed her. To me, it was pitiful to see a 'saint' die lying on a mat spread upon the damp earth, her feeble body covered with patched rags. There she passed away, and while I knelt at her side, the family recited the prayers for the dying. The funeral Mass was the next morning, in the room where she died. There was no coffin, no embalming. The body was merely wrapped in her mat, carried to a nearby hillside, and covered with sod."

In this same letter Father Sandy tells a whopper on himself, about a trip in the rainy season. "For a few hours it was not so bad, but as I proceeded on foot, the narrow paths of red clay became more and more unmanageable. Hollows became pools of water, slanting parts of the walk became extremely slippery, dikes filled up and overflowed, and in some places the water was ankle deep on the roadway. So, you see, it wasn't as easy as walking the paved road in front of Maryknoll. On my feet were a couple of old white gymnasium shoes with rubber soles and suction holes in the bottom which smacked and clucked at every step. The sole of the right shoe had been loosening all week during my constant walking on wet paths (we've seen the sun only twice in ten days), but this stick-in-the-mud walking finished it. So I had to take off my shoes and hoof it in the raw. And then my troubles began. The rain beat into my face and covered my glasses which are an indispensable part of my everyday adornment, and I wiped them off every twice in a while with the sleeve of my shirt. Unfortunately, I had left my handkerchief in my cassock pocket, and it was safely hidden away in one of the baskets. I was in my shirt sleeves because it is easier to walk this way—and the sleeves were handy, too, to wipe the pretty beads of 'per sweat' from my noble brow.

"Bare-foot walking is well-nigh universal in the villages

in this part of China, but my feet were not used to it, and I kept wondering how I managed so well during my happy barefoot days of childhood. Pebbles became needle points, and 'slide, Kelly, slide' was my frequent advice to myself. But the climax came when on a path less than a foot wide, and very muddy, I slipped and went head over heels into the flooded rice paddy a couple of feet below. Oh, how the Christians who were traveling with me roared with laughter. And as I picked myself up, I couldn't help joining them in their hilarity, for I was a sight. White clothes had become streaky brown, my hands had sunk in the slime up to my wrists, my face splashed in the muddy water, until I looked like I was ready for a minstrel show. I had 'lost face' as well as my balance. But then I was braced by a frequent expression of my mother:

> 'If ye fa,' dinna take time to rise,
> Just pick yerself up and run on.'

So I did just that, and I'm running, still."

Both in Fachow city and in the outlying farming villages, the influence and good will created by Holy Cross School began to be felt. In his constant trips around the parish, people began to ask Father Sandy about the Church, and what they must do to become a Lord of Heaven disciple. He had pushed his finger through the dike, and now he dug and scraped and tore the breach wider until the trickle became a flood. He opened three catechumenates in 1924, and the list of those seeking instruction in the doctrine became larger and larger.

That year a young Maryknoll missioner, Father Charles Walker, came out from America and was assigned to Fachow as Father Sandy's curate. Now that he had a lieutenant, he pressed the fight for converts on a double front.

He was successful in getting a group of merchants to begin their catechumenate—a sure sign of Father Sandy's extraordinary zeal, for this class in China is notoriously reluctant to take the painful step that often means giving up concubines and opium. Father Sandy knew, of course, that to catch these big fish in his net would give "face" to the Church; it would influence others to come into the fold and in general would give a Catholic tone and atmosphere to the business and social life of the whole city.

In January of Father Sandy's third year at Fachow the Red scare of the Twenties abruptly halted mission work all over the country. Communists had infiltrated into vital posts in the government following the Revolution of 1911, and Sun Yat-sen's founding of the Republic. With Chiang Kai-shek's rise to power, however, a purge was initiated to break the back of Moscow's influence. It was the Reds fighting for their political life that created the state of war. Troops of the two factions clashed in pitched battle in more than a hundred port cities along the eastern seaboard of China. Tsingtao was in turmoil. Canton was a battlefield.

An incident in January, 1925, touched off the fuse that lit the explosion of violent anti-foreign feeling of both warring parties. During a strike in Shanghai, English troops, in an effort to protect the property of British nationals, fired point blank into a crowd of rioters and killed three Chinese. No foreigner, by the single virtue of being a foreigner, was any longer safe in the country. The United States State Department instructed government officials in China to issue a warning that all American citizens, for their own protection, were to leave the country.

When this news reached Fachow Father Sandy was alone, Father Walker being in Hong Kong on retreat. There had been no fighting in Fachow at that time, so

Father Sandy did not give a second thought to the order to evacuate. A short time later, however, word came from the Maryknoll headquarters in Kongmoon that all missioners were to proceed to Hong Kong. Father Walsh, weighed down with the responsibility of both shepherds and sheep, decided that rather than jeopardize the work permanently by the loss of any of the missioners, the wiser course was to order the men to safety until the trouble blew over.

But then, a new problem arose. As the priests began arriving in Hong Kong it became evident that living quarters, facilities for saying Mass, and arrangements for meals in the Maryknoll house were totally inadequate. It was decided that a group of Maryknoll Fathers were to go on to Manila to accept the American Jesuits' proffered hospitality until the all-clear signal in China.

Father Sandy was one of the group that went to the Philippines. The visit was an eye-opener to him, and to all the exiled missioners. In the heart of the pagan Orient was a country as Catholic as Ireland, Spain, or Poland. The forced vacation with the Jesuits was Father Sandy's first holiday since going to China in 1920, but it was not a long one, for in October word came that it was now safe to return to China and to the mission parishes.

Father Sandy arrived at Fachow in late October. He immediately learned that the fighting had just started in his city. Running and hiding, and running back again to be at the side of his frightened flock, the missioner's own courage was an inspiration to the people. He has left us a full account of the confusion and terror of those days.

"On the seventh of November four thousand soldiers on the payroll of the Bolsheviks took Fachow after several days of fighting. We had a splendid view of the battle, staged on a hill to the south of the city wall. The 'Bolschys' kept up firing on the city for days, and nights, too. Sundown doesn't stop the noise of battle around this part of China.

"The poor people were very frightened, and with good reason, for no matter who wins, they are always the sufferers. They have to supply bed and board to the soldiers, and whatever else they demand.

"Refugees came to the mission, the men living in the school and the women taking over my place. We removed the Blessed Sacrament, and spent the days dodging bullets.

"Finally the city yielded and the local soldiers escaped to Shek Shing, thirty five miles south of Fachow, and left our walled city in the hands of the Bolsheviks.

"About the seventeenth of November, however, my friend, General Chan Choh-Ying, commanding those who had retreated from Fachow, returned with three thousand reinforcements, machine guns and cannon to retake the city. He meant business, too, if one can judge by the way he went about it. But the Bolsheviks sent to Kochow for more soldiers and in three days Chan Choh-Ying and our old home guard had to beat a retreat.

"On the twenty-fifth of November there was a young revolution in the Reds' camp when nearly one thousand soldiers refused to obey orders. I never saw a town shut up so quickly. The ferrymen anchored their boats, hundreds of people were forced to wade across the river, men and women were running with bundles and baggage. All was excitement. But the fighting was over and peace and order came back to Fachow."

Another disaster followed on the heels of war. In December there was a flood, followed by famine and epidemic, in the Fachow area. Father Sandy organized relief work. He built shelters for the homeless, and had soup lines for the starving people. He nursed the sick and buried the dead. He was everywhere and into everything during those days of terrible suffering, helping, consoling, and giving courage to the prostrate people.

Years after Father Sandy had moved away and the flood itself was forgotten, missioners continued to reap a great harvest of souls in Fachow because of the love and devotion of this apostle who was truly a "spiritual father" to his people.

Through January Father Sandy and his new curate, Father Gleason, pieced together and patched up the mission work so long and so violently interrupted by the tragedies of the past year. The school was reopened. Vocations to the priesthood were fostered. Catechumenates started again. Trips to the outlying villages went back on schedule. Father Sandy was a dynamo, burning with a restless and unquenchable zeal to bring more and more souls into the arms of Christ.

On Chinese New Year's new assignments came from Father Walsh at Kongmoon. Father Sandy received one. He was ordered to leave Fachow and go to the mission parish of Sunchong at the other end of the vicariate. Sunchong was then the most difficult post in the Maryknoll territory. Nestled in the rugged mountain district of Kwangtung Province, it lay in the heart of the bandit country. Only the challenge of "impossible" Sunchong and the promise of a new and greater fight eased the pain of parting in the heart of Father Sandy—a part of which great heart he left in Fachow forever.

... through fever, fire, famine

Nineteen hundred and twenty-six.

It was the year for trips and traveling. Norwegian explorer Amundsen's first air flight to the North Pole. The United States Marines to Nicaragua. American swimmer Gertrude Ederle's channel crossing. Lawrence of Arabia's march into the desert. And Father Sandy's Chinese junk voyage to Sunchong.

In the delta of the West River, at a point directly south of where it unites with the Pearl and gives up its name, the small but hostile market town of Sunchong stands guard at the crossroads of southern Kwangtung's rail and water routes.

The Catholic mission, with its compound in the town itself, reached out into the surrounding countryside until the whole parish made up an area the size of Delaware. It was to this place, dubbed "Missioners' folly" by priests who had worked there, that Father Sandy arrived from Fachow in the last week of February of his fifth year in China.

Father Joseph Sweeney, previous pastor of this parish, waited around in Sunchong to introduce Father Sandy to the people and the work, before moving on to take up a labor which eventually led to the foundation of one of the largest leper colonies in the Far East. Something of what the old pastor told the new one can be guessed at from a description of the Sunchong mission which Father Sweeney put in a letter written to the States in 1923. His tribute to the French missioner who pioneered this territory is glowing, but his description of the mission compound and a hint of the physical stamina needed by the pastor leave no doubt that the life he led there—and into which he was about to initiate Father Sandy—was rugged.

"Not long after Father Le Restif opened Sunchong he was stricken by the bubonic plague that raged in the place. God miraculously preserved him in that city of death. This real apostle, who is completely in love with the Chinese, is a linguist, an electrical and telegraphic expert, and a mathematician. Yet the big brain and the lion heart in no way roughened his childlike disposition."

And then the part about the mission compound. "Sunchong, being in the sharp angle of two rivers, and the mission having a creek on three sides, the house is damp even in the dry season, and during the floods it has water several feet in depth on the first floor. Our mission compound has three two-storied buildings built in a hollow square: a chapel, a residence, and a sort of hostelry or meeting place for the Christians. The front view at a distance looks prosperous on account of the heavy porches recently built to strengthen the unsteady walls. But the roofs of our buildings sag, the windows are falling out, and

the first typhoon may tumble down the walls. The chapel
is in such condition that my French predecessor did not
reserve the Blessed Sacrament, and we find ourselves
deprived of It also."

Father Sweeney's story continues: "Eight mission stations have been established. It requires a trip of two hundred and forty miles, most of it over foot paths, to reach
them. It is difficult to instruct the people not only because
they are widely scattered, but also because three different
and distinct dialects are spoken in the area."

The six-foot-four giant who became China's apostle to
the lepers, Father "Big Joe" Sweeney, concluded his report
about Sunchong with a pithy, tongue-in-cheek, typically
Oriental understatement: "Bandits are not entirely unheard of here."

Father Sandy found everything as Father Sweeney had
said it was. It did not dampen his spirits or make him
hesitate to tackle the tremendous job he had on his hands. He
went into a huddle with himself and called for the old
quarterback sneak play, "find a need, fill it, and cash in on
the results." One of the first things he did was to repair and
convert one of the two-story buildings on the mission property into a school. With the master's touch, acquired and
perfected in Fachow's Holy Cross, Father Sandy made a
success of his Sunchong school overnight. The people, who
at first had seemed reserved, even sullen, began to show
interest in a man and a Church obviously wanting to help
them.

The good will that the school created, however, did not
bring any tangible results. All of Father Sandy's efforts to
open a catechumenate in the city ended in failure. The strat-
egist decided upon a new course of action. In Fachow he
had worked from the city out into the country. But Sun-

chong was not Fachow. Father Sandy determined to train
his guns first on the farming districts and then fight his
way, village by village, back to the city.

The summer of 1926 was one long mission trip. He
worked out a plan of attack that combined his priestly care
of the Catholic families with his campaign to open new catechumenates in the pagan strongholds. An entry in his
mission diary, dated July 12, 1926, reveals not only his
method of operation but how successful it was.

"July 12th. Set out from Precious Jade village at ten in
the morning. Not rushing, arrived at White Pheasant as
the sun was going down. The eleven Catholic families gave
us a warm welcome, but everyone in the village seemed
happy to see us. The pagans outnumber the Christians by
at least twenty to one there. After the Catholic men and I
had supper together at Number Three Uncle's house, I
began questioning the wee ones in the catechism. I heard
all the confessions and followed them with night prayers and
the Rosary, and I preached on the Fourth Commandment. All
the Catholics were present but, of course, a million pagans, too. After taking the names and birth dates of the
three babies to be baptized after Mass the next morning, I
sat and chatted with the men until after midnight as the
women and children had disappeared to their homes. It is at
this time that I do my best propaganda work. For the
benefit of the pagan men present I told the story of St.
Paul's conversion, his falling off the horse and all. The
next morning at Mass I preached on the Blessed Sacrament. Then baptisms, and arrangements for a Catholic
wedding in August. I took my medicine bag and visited
every home where there was anyone sick. It was close to
eleven o'clock, by the sun, when I sat down for my breakfast of rice and soup. While I was eating, a delegation of

pagans came to talk with me. They had a list of twenty-three who wanted to study the doctrine. I asked them what prompted them to want to join the Church, and all seemed to agree it is the help we give to the sick. I told them that was good and that I would send a catechist to live in the village as soon as I returned to Sunchong city. I left for Stone Gate village about noon."

In October, Father Sandy got an assistant. Father Otto A. Rauschenbach, a Maryknoller from St. Louis, after a year of language study in Kongmoon, was assigned as curate to the Sunchong mission.

With the extra help in the school, and someone to assist him with the mission trips, Father Sandy decided to do something he had planned for a long time. He was going to open a dispensary at the mission. He had learned that caring for the sick made a deeper impression on the people than did his school, or the library he had started. He ordered three hundred dollars' worth of medicine from Hong Kong, and when the bundles arrived, the Sunchong "Lord-of-Heaven-Hall-Get-Medicine Shop" opened for business.

Father Sandy and Father Rauschenbach both had had a mission medicine course in the Seminary, as all Maryknollers had, so the two "doctors" were not complete "greenhorns" with a pill and a scalpel. They were swamped with work. People came from distant villages with all kinds of ailments. A pagan woman brought her two-year-old son, wasting away from malnutrition, to Father Sandy for help. A dose of santonin and calomel put color and life back into the boy in forty-eight hours. Father Rauschenbach did a successful eye-suture to save the sight of a fisherman who had been careless with his hooks. An old granny was cured of an ulcer on her foot that had been open and suppurating for more than two years. Father Sandy set a beggar's broken arm. The sick and the wounded and the diseased continued to come. The cures piled up and the fame of the spiritual fathers was broadcast all over three counties.

Most important of all, the dispensary was directly responsible for thirty-three adult baptisms in the first six months. The gentleness, care, and concern of the missioners for the sick and suffering won the heart of the city. Love begets love, and in this case love begot conversions. Father Sandy's dispensary, in which he practiced Christlike charity, was filling the Sunchong Catholic Church.

It was about that time that Father Sandy had his first encounter with the bandits of Sunchong. He had made the trip to Portuguese Macao to buy supplies and medicines, and had nearly reached home on the return journey when the fireworks began. At a bend in the river just outside the city—where the water was no deeper than a man's hips and the boats were forced to move slowly—a band of shooting, shouting men charged from the shore into the river and forced Father Sandy's junk to a halt. Bullets flew wildly, many drilling into the side of the junk. No one aboard was wounded but all were terrified. As the bandits, in complete control of the situation, began systematically to strip the boat and the passengers of everything valuable, Father Sandy stepped forward and introduced himself. The leader of the gang was taken completely by surprise at this development, and was quite obviously abashed. He mumbled apologies to Father Sandy and barked orders to his men to return everything they had taken and let the junk pass. Father Sandy, in glory, planted himself on deck and sailed into Sunchong a hero.

The victory was shortlived. A month later, on a visit to Kwong Hoi to meet Father Walsh, Father Sandy had reason to bolster his wavering faith in the reports of the ferocity of some bandits, if not Sunchong's.

It happened this way. Father Walsh and Father Sandy both arrived in Kwong Hoi the same night. At the Catholic mission, which had a caretaker but no resident priest, the two missioners met, exchanged news, cooked their own supper, and went to bed. At three in the morning bedlam broke loose. An army of bandits began shooting its way into the city. The defending soldiers fought off the invaders for an hour or so, but losing ground, they suddenly pulled out and retreated across the river. The city was left to the mercy of the bandits.

Near dawn the marauders, on a looting spree, got around to the mission, broke down the door, and led the priests, as prisoners, to the bandit chief. It was evening before the soldiers across the river mounted a counter-attack. When they did, the bandit chief made his two prisoners promise to return, and forced them to cross the river, under fire, to deliver his truce terms to the soldiers. The troops from the city had already lost too much face to be satisfied with a conditional surrender. When the two missioners explained that they had pledged on their honor to report back to the bandit chief, the officer in command not only forbade their return but placed them under arrest. The next day the soldiers recaptured the town, rounded up the bandits, and released their priest-prisoners.

When the whole affair ended, Father Sandy wondered if it weren't the missioners who had lost face. Father Walsh assured him that if they had, the finders were welcome to keep it. He advised returning home immediately with what they had left.

Back in Sunchong, the work continued. More catechumenates were opened, the school and the dispensary were running smoothly, the local bandits showed signs of friendliness. Father Sandy was with the people he loved, people who loved him. He was happy. Many evenings after a hot, hard day he would stroll down to the waterfront and sit with the farmers, coolies, and beggars to smoke and chat for a few hours. He would tell them of America and its locomotives, its hospitals, and its cathedrals. They would keep him abreast with the news and rumors that came in by "bamboo wireless" from all over the parish—who was sick, the day's price of rice in the market, what families were feuding. Off in the middle of China, half a world from Dix Street, Worcester, Father Sandy was at home and among his own.

On the eve of All Souls' day in 1928, Father Sandy made a mission trip into the country to say Mass for the deceased relatives and friends of his people on the Church's Memorial Day. At dawn he sang a Requiem High Mass, his choir of two catechists and a cook roaring out the Latin responses with more spirit than song. He was unvesting after the special ceremony of the absolution of the dead when the dizziness hit him. He had felt feverish on rising that morning but, thinking it just a touch of malaria, he had shaken off his loginess and gone on hearing confessions, and later preached at the Mass. But when he had finished the ceremony his head pounded, he felt weak and dizzy, and chills shook his whole body. Two or three men helped him to a bed and piled cotton quilts on him. He lay on a board bed in the little mud home, in and out of delirium for three days.

Before sunup on November 5, to catch the morning coolness, a thoroughly weakened Father Sandy managed to drag himself eight miles back to Sunchong. Father Rauschenbach put him to bed immediately. Unable to diagnose the case, he started the "shot gun" treatment— a dozen doses of different kinds of medicine, in the hope that one would hit the target. After four days Father Sandy protested that he was much better and insisted on getting up and going back to work. That same afternoon, when he was in the schoolyard joking with the children, he felt a strange wave of giddiness sweep over him. Then he collapsed.

Father Rauschenbach was desperately worried. He hired a sampan at once; and with so much help that the people were falling over one another, Father Sandy was carried to the river and made as comfortable as possible on the little boat. The trip to Kongmoon took thirty hours but Father Sandy seemed to hold up well. When the two priests arrived at their destination the next night, Father Rauschenbach enlisted half a dozen coolies to help him carry the patient to the Protestant clinic on the far side of town. With doctor's care, the right medicine, and good food, Father Sandy was back on his feet and off to Sunchong in a week.

But he was not over it yet. On the very day that Father Sandy arrived back at his parish, the dizziness attacked him again. Almost immediately he went into a coma. Again Father Rauschenbach hired a sampan, but this time he did not stop at Kongmoon. At that city he transferred Father Sandy to a steam launch and went on to Hong Kong.

Father Sandy lay in St. Paul's hospital, in the British colony, for five weeks. The doctors discovered he was suffering from severe sunstroke, complicated by quartan malaria. When he was finally discharged from the hospital he went to the Maryknoll Procure in Kowloon to rest and regain his strength before returning upcountry to his mission.

Father Ford came down from Kaying at that time. As Prefect Apostolic of the Kaying mission he was on his way to Rome to make his "ad limina" visit to the Holy Father. First, however, he planned to visit the new Maryknoll missions in Korea and Manchuria. When he met Father Sandy and learned of his long sickness, he insisted that the stubborn Scot take a vacation and go with him on the trip north. Father Sandy gave in, after some argument, and the two missioners booked passage on the *S.S. President Taft* to Kobe, Japan.

It was a wonderful six-week trip. The two travelers were welcomed and feasted by their brother missioners everywhere in the chain of Maryknoll mission outposts that then, in 1928, ringed the Orient.

They went from Kobe to Pusan in southern Korea, to Pengyang in the north, across the Yalu to Fushun and Dairen in Manchuria. Snatches from the diaries of the two priests read like the accounts of St. Paul's missionary journeys.

Father Sandy wrote: "The always crowded Catholic Mission at Antung, where Father Leo Davis is pastor, is proof enough why Korea is called 'Ireland of the Orient.' "

Father Ford made an entry datelined December, Hiken, Korea: "Monsignor Byrne's large and busy mission boasts of a church, a school, a clinic, a training center for women catechists, and an orphanage."

In Manchuria, Father Sandy observed: "These sturdy northerners seem better off in the material things of life than our people in the South. The houses are all of brick; there are no floods here; even the poor eat three meals a day. Somewhere in the writings of St. Augustine, or was it St. Thomas, there's a passage about the difficulty of getting people with no bread (or rice) for their bellies to become interested in spiritual food for their souls. This place is perfect proof of the saint's thesis. The people are prosperous and Monsignor Lane is herding them into the arms of Holy Mother Church."

The bracing northern climate, the respite from the worries and anxieties of caring for a large and scattered flock, and the contagiously happy companionship of Father Ford restored Father Sandy to complete health and to his old self—full of great strength and greater spirit. Once more he was restless in his eagerness to be in Sunchong, to be with his flock, to quench his burning thirst for more and more souls.

By that time Chiang Kai-shek had already gained undisputed control of the army and government of the infant Republic. The defeated Red forces, their bid for power smashed, were routed from their stronghold in Kiangsi and had begun their epic six-thousand-mile march into exile to the barren mountain province of Shansi. China was at peace. Under the Kuomintong, industry and commerce grew, railways and canals were built, and country schools and even institutions of higher learning sprang up across the nation. The government grafted the new spirit of democracy into the old trunk of Confucian culture. Christianity was lifted to a place of honor, and missioners from Europe and America were welcomed to China and enjoyed friendly and official recognition.

It was to such conditions that Father Sandy returned, his broken health completely restored and his missionary heart full of new and greater plans for the apostolate. The Shen Fu (Spiritual Father) of Sunchong picked up the threads where he had left off. During 1929 and 1930 Father Sandy enlarged the school in the city and sent teachers into each of the villages of the parish to open elementary grades for the children of the farming families. He brought Chinese Sisters from Canton to Sunchong to train a team of women cathechists for work in the country. He opened a small annex to the dispensary, that he might house the sick of the outlying villages who were brought on stretchers to the mission for prolonged treatment. He inaugurated new catechumenates in eight of the stations scattered along the two hundred and fifty mile belt that bound the parish together, and maintained an around the calendar catechumenate in the city itself.

Father Sandy trained well the succession of curates he had in those years—the zeal and know-how of the veteran missioner rubbing off on the tyros who in their turn moved on to other districts to open new mission parishes in the Maryknoll Vicariate.

In the fall of 1931 word came from New York that it was time for Father Sandy to interrupt his mission work to return to the States for the furlough that the constitutions of the Society offered every ten years to the priests overseas. There was a little Scottish mother back in America waiting for her son. Father Sandy, after ten years in China, left Sunchong and went to her.

. . . with Xavier

A mother's hug of welcome . . . old friends and scenes revisited . . . and then goodbyes that must do forever . . . a pilgrimage . . . a breeze across the heather in quiet Scottish gloaming . . . a shower of roses at Lisieux . . . the hush and love and peace of the cave of Massabielle at Lourdes . . . the catacombs and majesty of Rome . . . the sacred charge that linked his name to Sancian . . . his "fiat" at the word to walk and work and win with Xavier. The memories of months blended and blurred.

Father Sandy spent a full and happy, even busy, year at home with his mother and brothers and sisters. Old reunions, mission talks and sermons everywhere, the visits to places he had known—all these filled up the days of his furlough. And then the quick and harsh farewells that leaving brought. Yet he must be off, his "other" family called, and needed him.

In his longing to see his native Scotland and to visit the

shrines of the Continent, Father Sandy decided to return to the Orient by way of Europe. He left New York a few days after Christmas, 1931, for Glasgow. He spent a few days there to start a heap of memories this trip was building up for all his future years. Hurried calls at Lisieux, Lourdes, and Rome. At each he left his prayers for China, and took away with him a new and stronger dedication to his own Chinese.

At Genoa Father Sandy boarded a Japanese freighter to make the trip East through the Suez Canal and on around the coast of India toward "home" and his new assignment.

In Hong Kong the news of his mission appointment was awaiting him. The words were there, yet he held his breath in unbelieving happiness. He read again; "To Sancian." He said the name in whispered joy, then shouted it —"Sancian!" This was the end of all his pilgriming. The shrine of shrines was soon to be his home. The place where fever and a thirst for souls killed Xavier. Perhaps somehow, someway the Saint would make a tool of his successor to bring about the final conquest of the people of the island. If it took pain, and agony, and even blood, Father Sandy offered his own to China's blessed Intercessor to win in time and for eternity the children and their children's children of the oldest race on earth.

In those first hours of his appointment Father Sandy felt he knew the part that he must play in the story of the Saint and the history of the place. And yet, the things a man feels most—the length and breadth and height of all his dreams and all his love—when he is forced to tell and speak them even to himself, they become confused and wary of commitment. That was the way with Father Sandy. He hardly dared, in the silence of his apostolic heart, to talk to God or even to himself of all the holy hopes he had and of the final sacrifice he freely offered for the crowning of his priesthood and his mission—as Xavier had before him.

The preparations for the trip did not take long. Some shopping for the things a man would need and couldn't get on an isolated island—candles, pipe tobacco, catechisms, quinine—things like that. Then, having booked passage on a motor launch to the mainland market-port across from Sancian, Father Sandy started off. The trip was like a thousand other trips that he had taken before, but it was different by the happy reason of its final destination.

It was a cold, raw Kwangtung day in middle February when the island's new pastor finally transferred at Kwonghai to an outsized sailing sampan and headed east across the choppy bay to Sancian. As the flimsy, bobbing, flat-bottom boat crept close to the black hump in the sea, Father Sandy slid out from under the wicker shelter that served as a cabin, and stood on the narrow, stubby deck, straining against the whipping spray to see the chapel steeple that he knew was there. Nearer, nearer, then he made it out. There it stood, half way up a rising, barren hill like some giant warrior facing China, his gleaming sword pointed to the sky. That was the shrine, the first lonely, unknown grave of the greatest apostle the world had known since Peter, Paul and Patrick.

There was no one on the shore to meet Father Sandy, but he was glad. He paid the fare that he had bargained for; the sampan turned and sailed away; and he was alone. He left his baggage on the beach and climbed the steep rock incline that led up to the concrete chapel's stairway. As he reached the porch platform in front of the shrine church he could see that the walls were cracked and sagging, the windows paneless, and the warped door stuck open at a crooked angle. He went inside. The wind whistled through the little oratory, and he pulled his cotton jacket up around his neck. He dropped to his knees and knelt for a long time praying and thinking and dreaming of what his life had come to, of where he was, and what it meant, and why, of all the men on earth, God had chosen him for this.

To this island, to this very spot, four centuries before, another missioner had come and knelt to pray the prayers and think the thoughts and dream the same dreams that were racing and crashing through Father Sandy's head.

The story goes—it is history now—that a young and dashing Spaniard from a castle in Navarre had gone to Paris to study the ways of life and love and luxury. But he was blocked and detoured in his quest by the nagging of a fool who talked only of God and of souls and of martyrdom. The young man held out, but for only a short and angry time. Then in the victory of the fool, folly found a twin.

The story leaps and bolts from there until the day a master sends a son across the world to conquer it for Christ. In March, 1541, in obedience to Ignatius Loyola, Founder of the Society of Jesus, at the command of Paul III, Supreme Pontiff of Christendom, under the patronage of John III, King of Portugal, and with his own compulsive thirst for souls driving him on, Francis Xavier left Europe to evangelize the East.

The overwhelming, almost universal, fantastic vastness of this commission could only be known and marveled at when the apostle lay dying from the exhaustion of his very accomplishment of it. The first half of his apostolic conquest had brought him to Goa and down around the southern bend of India to Cochin and Colombo, eastward across the Indian Ocean to Malacca and the Moluccas, back through the Java Sea to the Celebes. Those sallies into the heart of pagan Asia were not merely for reconnaissance, to chart a map for later days. Francis Xavier had won and secured a South Asia perimeter for the defense of the Faith in the Orient by stationing an army of sentries, baptized by himself, along the line of march.

With more than half of Francis' allotted time already spent, he hastened up along the China coast to Kagoshima and Hirado, in Japan. The permanency of the trail Xavier blazed in the southern port cities of the Japanese Empire was tested and proven in the great persecution that followed his own death. In the district of Shimabara alone, 40,000 Christians were wiped out to the last man, woman, and child for the Christian Faith.

Xavier knew that to win Japan was not enough. The hub and heart of the Orient was the Imperial Court of China. If he could plant the cross in that core, the shadow of it would fall across all Asia. Xavier's plan was to enter China from the south and work his way up to Peking by the inland route. It was this daring strategy that brought the apostle eventually to Sancian. It was on that island, the stepping stone to the mainland, while waiting for a boat to carry him to the consummation of his dreams, that Francis Xavier was overcome by a great fever, and died.

The struggle for the remainder of the Orient was not without battles won, but the total victory was denied. By the armistice of Xavier's death, the final triumph was postponed until the campaigns of future missioners were undertaken.

The world has seldom seen, and may not often see again, such love, such thirst for souls, such total immolation as that which was Francis Xavier's. Still that day on cold, barren Sancian, in the chapel that marked the sacred ground of the Saint's dying, another fire was lit. The heart and soul of Father Sandy, kneeling there, had come ablaze. He gave his all and took what he was given—the apostolic model of the life and death of Xavier. . . .

Climbing down to the beach, Father Sandy gathered up

his bags and baskets and took the broader path that led around the hill. He saw some shops ahead, and heard a baby crying. As he came nearer to the market place he saw some men. He called to them, and they came running.

"Ah, Spiritual Father, what is your honorable clan name?

"Oh, the great clan of Ka!

"Is Ka Shen Fu going to stay here?

"Good, good. We are very happy because Shen Fu is surely a most kind man.

"What is Ka Shen Fu's honorable age?

"Truly? One would believe that Ka Shen Fu is much older. Ka Shen Fu has great intelligence and learning for such a young man.

"Is Ka Shen Fu a 'Beautiful Country' person?

"New York. Good, good. Some of us have heard of Ka Shen Fu's honorable place of origin."

"We talked and talked," wrote Father Sandy later, "until I think I learned as much about my new parish as the people learned about their new pastor."

As the facts came firing in at him, Father Sandy tried to sort and store them up for future easy use. Population 6,000, a little more or less . . . 1500 Catholics . . . 40 clan villages . . . unhulled rice measured "old weight" for barter . . . no scheduled market days . . . island, end to end distance, 50 li, crosswise, 12-15 li . . . two lepers on the hill beyond Flying Sand Village . . . a haunted cave . . .

Father Sandy broke away and climbed the hill that led to the mission church and his new home. The Sancian parish center was perched on the top of a rocky hill about a mile from the beach. Father Sandy was to come to know that it was a cold, windy walk up and down the hill in winter, and a broiling hike in summer. There was a church, a

school, a dispensary, and a priest's house. It was from that
four-in-one, mud-brick building that Father Sandy looked
out across the land and ruled his island kingdom.

His new dedication at the shrine and his fresh urgency
to follow Xavier, propelled Father Sandy into a whirl-
pool of activity. His first task was to count the sheep. Their
needs, their weaknesses, their strength, these must be
known before he could cement his apostolic plans for
winning all of Sancian.

The newly arrived pastor mapped out a route to follow
in the visitation of the island's clan villages. With his Mass
kit, a basket full of doctrine books, and his medicine bag,
he made the first day's stop, and then the next's and on
around the circuit through the forty settlements. From
Sandy Lake, from Great Waves, from North Hollow—from
all forty of them he came away with wounds so deep that
he seemed too weak to suture them, or even to care about
the bleeding.

It was the unexpected shock, the sudden completeness of
the crash that crushed Father Sandy. He stood and stared
in agony at the splinters of his broken holy hopes, the
disenchanted apostolic dreams he believed he had glued
with Xavier's zeal. There was no hiding nor turning from
the sight of it. It was defeat before the fight. In a word—
there was no flock!

There were no sheep. Sancian was a church on paper
only. A farce. The plan to drown a man in the pool of his
own digging. They had told him of 1500 Christians. That
was the count they gave. But some evil trickery had
multiplied his lambs and sheep to mountainous distortion.
In all of Sancian, testing every head in every village, the
seal of faith was worn by only fifteen souls.

Father Sandy climbed the hill where he had knelt before,
and on the spot where Xavier also lost his flock, he re-

ceived the grace to see and know that he was closer than ever to his sainted predecessor.

With the resiliency and bounce that Father Sandy always had, and which had increased from practice, he began all over again. This time he concentrated first of all on the schools. He had one in the mission compound and another in his farthest village. He hired an additional teacher for each and bought new books for the pupils. Then he opened a third school in New Earth Village.

Hand in hand with the mission's educational program went the dispensary work. He welcomed the sick. Not only at the center did he receive them but at the call of Catholic or pagan he hurried out six, twelve, twenty li to be with them and help.

With each new method he tried, with each new avenue he entered, Father Sandy worked and slaved and prayed to protect and strengthen his tiny flock by building a sheltering wall for them with the souls of new and "other" sheep. At the end of his first year in Sancian, Father Sandy sent his *status animarum* report to newly consecrated Bishop Walsh in Kongmoon, and scribbled in the margin: "From 15 to 38 in twelve months is a victory, of course, but not a very big one. We are making progress, however, and soon we may get the 1400 apostates back."

In constant pursuit of those 1400 islanders who had given up the Faith in the priestless days before Sancian was joined to the Maryknoll Vicariate, Father Sandy tried a hundred unsuccessful ways to win them. One night at his beads, however, he hit upon a plan that was more than just a distraction. He got the idea of repairing the chapel shrine down by the beach and organizing a huge pilgrimage from Hong Kong and Macao to Sancian. He would bring in outsiders to pray and profess their faith for all of his stiff-necked 1400 to see. The more he thought of it, the more was he convinced that it could be the tool to open up their hearts.

In the spring of 1933 the renovation of the Memorial Chapel was begun. Father Sandy brought down from Hong Kong a contractor to oversee the job. The outside of the shrine chapel was plastered with white cement. The roof was repaired and reinforced with concrete. The empty tomb itself, and the stone slab placed there in 1609 were stuccoed with a terrazo-like finish. The stone steps leading from the beach to the porch of the memorial oratory were given the necessary repairs. Then Father Sandy directed the building of a cement finished rock pier jutting out some 200 feet into the bay to receive the flotilla of barges, launches, junks and sampans which he could already envision coming up the bay to Sancian.

Everything was finished. The date of the pilgrimage was set for December 9. The call had been sent to Hong Kong and Macao, and Father Sandy was ready to receive the pilgrims—and he hoped and prayed that his 1400 were ready, too.

December on Sancian can be a raw, biting 40 degrees, but December 9 dawned clear and calm. On the morning of the great day . . . but Father Sandy, in a letter back to Maryknoll, New York, wrote minute by minute details of those sacred hours of the pilgrimage.

"The *Hay Ning* came into sight, up the bay, at 7:00 A.M. This was the chartered steamship which brought most of the 550 pilgrims from Hong Kong and Macao. The *Hay Ning* was flanked by two motor launches, four junks, and a dozen sampans. It was a thrilling sight to see this armada coming nearer and nearer to our island.

"The pilgrims transferred to sampans to come ashore, for the water was not high enough for the *Hay Ning* to approach the pier. By eight o'clock all had assembled, in-

cluding thirty-six priest pilgrims, at the tomb for the opening prayers. Solemn Mass was at 9:00 A.M. By this time
many of the islanders had joined the crowds, and while it
is certain they were impressed by the seriousness and devotion of the pilgrims, we can only ask that the good God
make some of it rub off on them.

"There were three sermons: Chinese, Portuguese, and
English. Again prayers at the tomb and then a rest for
refreshments. At 1:00 P.M. all the pilgrims and about five
hundred of our people made the outdoor Way of the Cross.
Many followed the Stations in bare feet on the rocky path.
At 2:00 P.M. the *Hay Ning* was to leave Sancian to head
back to Macao and Hong Kong. After the Way of the
Cross, however, so many of the pilgrims stopped to say
private prayers at the shrine that departure was delayed
thirty or forty minutes.

"Our fondest dream had come true—to see a large crowd
of pilgrims come to Sancian to honor our Saint, and in so
honoring him, to wake up the islanders to their neglected
treasure. St. Francis Xavier must have been pleased by
it all—his unworthy successor surely was. Now, our Saint
must bring fruit out of the pilgrimage. He must touch the
hearts of the 1400."

In the days following the pilgrimage the people all over
the island were talking about the crowds that had come to
pray and to honor St. Francis Xavier. Father Sandy knew
that he must strike at once. If he was to do anything ef-
fective in the way of follow-up on the events of December 9,
he knew he must set out on a full circuit swing of Sancian,
visiting every village, hamlet, and home.

Immediately after Christmas he started off. Even in
thoroughly pagan districts he stayed overnight and said
Mass and preached to the people. Father Sandy always felt,
and often said, that any town would be a better place if

Christ even so much as passed by. So it was that in pagan villages the priest was alone with his God, saying Mass for them and for their conversion. What he looked for most on this trip was the sign of any change, any crack in the cold, hard mask the apostates wore when Christ or Christ's apostle came near. The exhausting march that took nearly seven weeks to complete most certainly did some good, sowed some seed, but to Father Sandy's straining, anxious eye nothing immediate or obvious occurred among the 1400.

To many of the mission stations on the island parish it was far shorter and much quicker to travel along the coast by boat than over the rocky paths of up-and-down hilly Sancian. It was by boat that Father Sandy, more often than not, did travel to these places. But the inconvenience and delay of hiring a sampan at the unexpected and unlikely hours that sick calls always seem to pop up, set Father Sandy to thinking and planning how he might get a boat of his own. The scheming Scot later admitted the strategy he used to get his navy. "A little prayer and plenty of hints to the right people."

His prayers and hints scored doubly. In 1933 Father Sandy blessed his little "fleet": *The Crusader,* an 18-foot skiff with sail and motor, and the *Star of the Sea,* a two-ton, 33-foot motor launch with a glass-enclosed cabin.

The acquisition of the boats opened a whole new apostolic field to Father Sandy. On the neighboring island, called Lower Sancian, the pastor knew that there were two large clan villages with a total population in excess of a thousand persons. The people on the main island had insisted to him over and over again that Lower Sancian was a rough and lawless place, that its people years earlier had half beaten to death a French missioner who had gone to them to preach the Gospel. Father Sandy laughed at all these tales, and now that he was captain of his crew, he determined to make the trip to Lower Sancian.

On a clear June morning the pastor, the head catechist, and the mission cook of Sancian, shoved off in *The Crusader* and headed south to the lower island. It was not a hazardous trip nor even a long one, but Father Sandy felt the excitement of one going into battle, and the pounding of his apostolic heart at the thought of a new conquest for Christ.

They arrived at Lower Sancian before noon, and tying up their boat, the three men walked up the beach until they saw the market place. Father Sandy well remembered the scene and later wrote of it: "At our appearance in the shopping center, the 'bamboo wireless' informed, what surely must have been, the island's entire population of the strange happening—a foreigner had arrived on their island. In a couple of twinklings the clans foregathered. Fifty good men and true! And such a barrage of questions. 'Who, what, when, where, and why' did not begin to cover them all.

"They invited me to stay overnight, which was just what I had hoped for; and I answered that I would if they allowed me to say Mass and preach to them in the morning—which they were delighted to do. So, I was all set.

"To these fifty men I gave my life history 'up to now;' the story of Christ, our Lord; of the one true Church; of the Church in China; the life and death of St. Francis Xavier; the Ten Commandments; and the significance of the Mass that I would celebrate in the morning. In return, they asked intelligent questions and it was a pleasure to talk with them.

"The next day, at dawn, I set up the altar under a picture of Sun Yat-sen, and with at least 200 people present, began Mass. I preached of Christ's birth and all listened with great interest. Afterwards, they treated me to a banquet breakfast and begged me to come back soon. I felt as St. Francis Xavier himself must have often felt, as I left Lower Sancian in a blaze of glory."

Father Sandy did go back. He opened a school there and, eventually, a catechumenate. The Church grew on the island and each year thereafter the pastor of the two-island parish conducted a spring and winter catechumenate for the fishermen and their families on Lower Sancian.

Just as Xavier's victories in India and Japan never made his failure to reach China a total defeat, so Father Sandy's triumph on the little island forever forestalled his frustration on Sancian from being branded a final rout. Father Sandy fought on. Results were slow to show, yet they were there. A glance at a few entries he scratched into the Sancian mission diary in 1937 and 1938 have a meaning all can appreciate.

"After Midnight Mass, firecrackers exploded all around the mission yard. Then chicken rice gruel was served to the cold and hungry men, women, and 'wee ones' who had walked many miles in the dark of night to receive Jesus into their hearts and bodies in Holy Communion, who had come to confess their love and faith in the Child of Bethlehem."

". . . Last week I took to the road. Sunday I walked 10 miles. Monday I walked 26 miles. Wednesday I walked 15 miles. Friday I walked 5 miles. Saturday I walked 15 miles. I guess you can say the mission trips on Sancian make a 'miler-aire' out of a man."

". . . Today there are 187. Much better than our first Easter on Sancian when there were only 15 to say 'Amen' to the prayers."

In his victories, as well as in his defeats on Sancian, Father Sandy with the mind of Xavier kept one truth, one conviction firmly rooted in his priestly soul—to be a missioner is to pioneer the wilderness. Were he able but to blaze the trail, others, he felt certain, would follow to build a highway for God across the face of Sancian, across the separating water of the bay, across the length and breadth of China.

. . . to victory

Men judge that it's the death of a hero which gives glory to his life, but God judges rather that the life of His apostle gives victory to his death. Whatever be the world's judgments, it was God's that Father Sandy's apostolic life merited the victory of a martyr's death. And that victory was near.

In October, 1938, Father Sandy left Sancian and his island parish in the keeping of his new curate, Father John T. Joyce, of Kew Gardens, N. Y., the latest Maryknoll arrival in China. Father Cairns himself had to make the trip to Hong Kong to buy medicines for his dispensary, to have his eyeglasses checked, and to get a few days' vacation. The date of that trip—indeed, the trip itself—proved to be important in the light of all that was to follow.

China, through the nineteen thirties, was threatened by the growing strength of the military might of Japan. In 1931 the Japanese staged the Mukden "incident" in Manchuria. The episode not only pitted Chinese troops against an aggressor, but triggered an explosion that blew the whole world into the greatest war in history. The Japanese took Shanghai in November, 1937. A month later Nanking fell. Japan rapidly pushed its lines forward. After a little more than a year of full scale invasion, Japanese armies reached Kwangtung Province in South China. Chiang Kai-shek's forces fought fiercely to save Canton, provincial capital of Kwangtung, but the defenders were finally overpowered and the city capitulated to the Japanese military machine in October. Canton was a shambles. The wounded and homeless wandered the streets dazed and starving. Refugees piled into the city from all directions to avoid the path of war. The Japanese troops billeted themselves in Canton's five Catholic orphanages and pushed the children out on the street to swell the number of destitute.

It was at that time that Father Sandy, in Hong Kong on his shopping trip, decided to return to Sancian by way of Canton to see whether there was any way he could assist in the relief work there. Bishop Fourquet of Canton welcomed Father Sandy and put him to work immediately rounding up the refugees into camps, and going out to the country to seek rice for the starving. After three weeks, although he saw that his help was still desperately needed in the relief work, Father Sandy felt he should return to his own flock on Sancian. Bishop Fourquet, however, appealed to him to stay longer and offered to make arrangements with Father Sandy's own Bishop in Kongmoon that he might carry on the desperately needed relief work.

The pitiful plight of so many thousands of poor and suffering people forced Father Sandy to agree to stay on a while longer. In the tragic atmosphere there was one incident, connected with Bishop Fourquet's obtaining permission to keep Father Sandy with him, that gave the Bishop, Father Sandy himself, and all who heard of it, a great

laugh. It happened over the wording of the telegram sent
to Kongmoon. "Request Cairns remains Canton," the
Bishop had wired. The Maryknollers, believing that the
cryptic message was informing them that Father Sandy had
been killed in the fighting then going on outside the city of
Canton, telegraphed back: "Dispose of Cairns' remains as
you think best." When the hilarious mistake was finally
straightened out, Father Sandy received the permission
that Bishop Fourquet wanted for him. He remained in
Canton to continue the work in the refugee camps.

The Bishop of Canton appointed Father Sandy temporary pastor of Our Lady of Lourdes Church to give him
some official standing in the eyes of the Japanese officials.
The new pastor was never hindered in his relief work by
the civil or military occupation forces. Others who were
also engaged in feeding and clothing the war victims were
constantly amazed at Father Sandy's fearlessness in con-
tinuing the work, even after the Japanese became openly
hostile to foreigners assisting the Chinese.

An Irish Jesuit who was in Canton at that time engaged
in similar refugee work wrote to a Maryknoller in Hong
Kong about Father Sandy's cool courage under fire.

"To us, watching on the side lines, Father Sandy led a
charmed life. Where other men tip-toed, he stomped.
Where others went out of their way to avoid incidents with
the occupying forces, Father Sandy seemed to invite them.
And yet, he was never arrested, beaten, or even humiliated
by the soldiers. Strange to say, the more he trod on their
toes, the more they seemed to like him. He alone, of all
those doing relief work, seemed to be able to get permission from the reluctant Japanese military. It was said
that he was the only one who could dare joke with them,
and an eyewitness once saw him slap a Japanese officer on
the back by way of greeting.

"Only those who saw him in action could appreciate the contribution he made to the enormous task. Once when the hungry mob even tore his clothes in their frenzy to get food, he merely smiled and said: 'If I were as hungry as they are, maybe I would not have the strength to be able to tear anyone's clothes.'

"Once I asked him how he felt as he traveled the local rivers and markets searching for quantities of rice for the refugees. Actually this was much more dangerous than living with the Japanese because it brought him into the 'no-man's land' between the enemy and the Chinese—a veritable target range for both sides. His answer was: 'I have never experienced the feeling of fear in my life. I can go anywhere and never feel the least bit nervous about danger.' "

Father Sandy agonized to see such suffering all around him. He spent himself to exhaustion helping the poor, the sick, the frightened. The city was a sea of pain. There was inflation. Industries closed down. The hungry and starving roamed the streets looking for food. In that early part of 1939 more than a hundred Chinese were found dead of starvation every day on the city streets.

Three times Bishop Fourquet requested Maryknoll to extend Father Sandy's stay in Canton, and each time word came back from Kongmoon granting the request. Father Sandy was the backbone of the refugee work, the wall his co-laborers leaned on when they themselves staggered from exhaustion.

The refugee camps housed and fed 20,000 people daily. Where Bishop Fourquet got the money for charity on such a colossal scale was a miracle never discovered. But the time came when the last penny had been spent, when everything that could be sold was gone, and when all the sources for getting more money had dried up. It was in December,

1940, just a little over two years from the time Father
Sandy had arrived in the prostrate city to begin the work,
that he was forced to end it. With a heart heavy at his own
helplessness to relieve the hopeless fate of so many thousands of sick and starving, he dragged himself out of Canton, and headed home to Sancian.

Father Sandy made his way to Cheung Chow, a small
island twelve miles south of Hong Kong, to take passage
on a junk going down the coast to Kwong Hoi, the market
port on the mainland across from Sancian. He was a long
and weary month on that island, waiting to secure a daring
junk captain who was willing to run the Japanese blockade. When he did contact such a captain and had made
arrangements for the voyage, there was another delay because of weather—a great calm settled on the harbor waters
for two days and two nights. Finally a favorable wind came
up and Father Sandy's junk made its dash out to sea.

They had not sailed an hour's distance from the island
when a Japanese gunboat scared them back to Cheung
Chow. The next night, joined by nine other junks to form
a ragged fleet, they successfully made it to the open sea
and headed south. It was a voyage full of peril, with the fear
of Japanese and pirates ever riding with them. Again, there
is a Father Sandy's account to tell us of it.

"Danger overshadowed the trip to Kwong Hoi; of the ten
junks in the convoy the Japanese captured and burned one.
Pirates fired on us, but the sailors rowed so energetically in
the calm sea that we escaped without a casualty or loss of a
single thing. During the excitement and shooting I stayed on
deck behind a sheet of iron and enjoyed the show. At
Kwong Hoi I went ashore, then boarded a small sailing
sampan for Sancian. After nearly two months of waiting,
and starting, and stopping, and detours, I arrived at Sancian
on February 28. Father Joyce was delighted to see me, and

I was happy to be home with him again after an absence of two years."

The two priests exchanged the years of news that each had to tell the other. Father Joyce's report on the progress made in the parish delighted the pastor's heart. There had been seventy-four adult baptisms, and some fifty of the 1400 strays of the fold had returned. The school was going well. Lower Sancian had its own chapel and a new catechumenate had just been opened there. And the war! Father Sandy told of his experiences, of his overwhelming anguish of heart caused by the suffering people in Canton, and of the high adventure of his trip home. Father Joyce told of the three harmless visits of Japanese reconnaissance teams to the island. He explained to Father Sandy that the food supply of the islanders was very low and that, for the last month or so, no sampan had dared to run the Japanese blockade to bring supplies from the mainland. The situation was grave. Poor Sancian. Poor China.

The two priests said the Rosary together that night for their flock, for all the 450,000,000 Chinese. On the fourth day of Father Sandy's return to Sancian the Novena of Grace began—those nine days in March set aside yearly in Catholic communities around the world to beg God for some special grace through the intercession of St. Francis Xavier. Father Sandy, at dawn each day of the Novena, walked the mile-long path down to the shrine chapel on the beach to say Mass at the Tomb and to fill again the need and want he had to soak up every mood and move and thought of Xavier.

The conquering Japanese armies had rolled south from Canton down through Kwangtung Province, and by the middle of March, Kwong Hoi, fifteen miles across the channel from Sancian, fell into their hands with very little resistance. On the 22nd, Sancian itself had a dress re-

hearsal of invasion. Father Sandy was off on the far side of
the island on a sick call. Father Joyce was at the mission
center. Around noon a Japanese motor launch pulled up
into the waters off Sancian. No sampan from the island
went out to meet it and two sailors from the launch were
forced to swim ashore. They commandeered a small boat
and returned to the ship to haul a squad of men to the
beach. Four snappily uniformed naval officers came toward
the mission. A dog barked. They shot it dead. They
reached the gate, brushed by Father Joyce, and looked
around the compound. Then they left.

In the meantime, however, more and more sailors had
put ashore. In small groups they began an inspection
tour of the shops and homes along the water front. In a
routine search of one of the shops the sailors found a gun
and some bullets. They collared the shopowner and fired
questions at him. Panicky at his inability to make himself
understood by the Japanese, he managed by bowing and
pointing, and bowing some more, to lead the sailors to the
mission. The Chinese hoped to draw the attention of his
captors from himself to the priests' house in the belief that
one of the Shen Fu's could clear up the matter. Father
Joyce, of course, knew no Japanese and could not give any
help to the thoroughly terrified shopkeeper. The sailors,
however, interpreted the whole maneuver as implicating
Father Joyce in the matter of the gun and bullets. One of
them began shouting and roaring at the priest in Japanese.
Then, this same sailor spat out in English, "Kill, kill."

Convinced that the lad was bluffing, Father Joyce began
to walk toward the house. The sailor yelled something at
the priest. Father Joyce turned around and saw the
Japanese load his rifle and point it at him. He tried to pray.
The sailor fired. The bullet grazed Father's cassock, but did
not hit him. That was all.

Later, when telling the story to Father Sandy, Father Joyce could not decide whether it was all a bluff or not, but he did tell him one thing of which he was certain—he had said the "Grace Before Meals" instead of the "Act of Contrition" at the last moment before the gun went off.

On Pentecost Sunday Sancian got another taste of what was to come. Three Japanese gunboats anchored off shore and poured shells on the island for two and a half hours. No one was killed, but there was plenty of property damage and the whole population of Sancian knew they were in a very one-sided war.

In May Father Joyce received an assignment to a new mission on the mainland. Sadly he left the shrine, the pastor, and the people he loved. Father Sandy was alone and the extra work that fell to him left him little time for anything but his prayers. There were the mission trips and sick calls, the school, the daily work in the dispensary, the new catechumenate on Lower Sancian—all these filled up his days and nights.

The Japanese situation was serious, of course, but Father Sandy, never knowing fear, could not bring himself to worry about the future. His people needed him then more than ever, and he stayed close to them and was a father to them in everything.

The Japanese continued looting, bombing, and strafing Sancian sporadically during May and June. In July and August, however, the tempo was stepped up, and the frequency of the attacks prompted Father Sandy to register a protest to the Japanese occupation government in Canton. He wrote a letter and took it to a shopkeeper who had mysterious ways of getting things off and on the island.

"Gentlemen," Father Sandy wrote, "Sancian Island was the first place in South China to be taken by the Japanese over three years ago. After three weeks here, your ships and men abandoned it, perhaps because it is too poor a place and there is nothing of value on the whole poverty-stricken island.

"Since I returned here, within the last year, your ships have come and burned the small boats of the poor Sancian fishing people. Your airplanes have dropped bombs, and one of your men stood Father Joyce in front of the church and shot at him.

"Food cannot be transported to the island, and the people need it. They are not fighting nor opposing you. They merely wish to live. You took the island three years ago. It's yours. Why kill and destroy on your own island?"

Father Sandy waited in vain for a reply. He wrote again and again and again. He felt that it was his duty to his people to be their spokesman. As he was an alien of a neutral country, and his own work and concerns were purely religious, he felt that he had a better chance of being heard, if the Japanese would listen at all, than had any of his Chinese flock. Yet inside of him, with his sound good sense and level-headed holiness, Father Sandy was surely as well aware as any saint or scholar could be that things were rushing to an end that made it paramount to be prepared by faith and hope and love.

What are the thoughts of such a man at a time like that? One may never dare to think of calling himself a martyr, yet a man can look ahead and see the possibility of being summoned to die for God and souls, or for loyalty to both. Only when a man has seen that vision, has been brought to the very brink itself, can he guess the thoughts that raced up and down in Father Sandy's head shortly before the end.

There is a way, however, for a person to get inside of Father Sandy. If one takes the prayer Father Cairns prayed, which was written by his earliest tutor in China, Bishop

Ford, and says it with the kind of love that moved the au-
thor-martyr to write it, then he could come close to Father Sandy at Sancian and guess what lay ahead at Sancian,
and feel what Father Sandy felt as his days rushed to an
end.

"Grant us, Lord, to be the doorstep by which the multitudes
may come to worship Thee. And if in the saving of their souls
we are ground under foot, and spat upon, and worn out, at least
we shall have served Thee in some small way in helping pagan
souls. We shall have become the King's Highway in pathless
China."

Father Sandy, in spite of the ever increasing danger of
traveling around the bombarded island, continued his mission trips and answered every call for medicine and com-
fort. The danger of those days drew the sheep and shepherd
closer. They needed him, and his own life would be mean-
ingless without them.

On December 9, 1941, Japanese soldiers and their camp
followers began making thieving raids on the mission in
broad daylight. Father Joseph P. Lavin, Father Sandy's
nearest Maryknoll neighbor, had been making frantic efforts
to communicate with the Sancian pastor to let him know of
the outbreak of war. During those dangerous days, a few
boats managed to run the Japanese blockade from Sancian
to the mainland, but none ever went the other way—from
the mainland to Sancian. It was from the captain of one
of the Sancian sampans that made it through to the mainland that Father Lavin learned what was happening on the
island. He wrote to tell Bishop Paschang, in Kongmoon,
the news he had heard.

"The raiders went immediately to the women's catechumenate building but were unable to enter because the doors
were locked and barred. Father Sandy hastened over from

his house and with characteristic courage he upbraided them. Father Sandy refused to let them enter, but covered by guns he was rendered helpless. He agreed to open the door if the marauders would agree to permit the women and children who were being instructed there to return home without harm. The Japanese agreed, and the women and children left—to run to the hills instead of to their homes. The women catechists, at Father Sandy's whispered urging, soon followed them.

"After removing all things from that building, the Japanese went to the priests' house, forced their way in, and removed everything of value. Under the conditions Father Cairns, of course, was helpless. The outside kitchen received the same treatment. At dark, the invaders entered the church. The sacristy was locked and they didn't break down the door because of the darkness. They promised to return to finish the job on another day. Father Cairns was fortunate because the sacred vessels and vestments were in the sacristy. The Japanese raiders forced the local people for four hours to carry the stolen goods to their motor boats."

Father Lavin had been unable to get a letter to Father Sandy. There was no other way possible to inform him that the United States and Japan were now at war.

On December 11, the Japanese looters returned and started their pillaging where they had left off the last day. Again on the 13th, the Japanese went to the mission to make the last check to be sure that in their previous raids, they had not overlooked anything worth stealing.

It was on that 13th of December, after the Japanese soldiers had left the mission compound, that Father Sandy saw an officer furtively make his way back up the hill. The priest went to meet him at the gate. The worried-looking soldier wore the insignia of a colonel. He bowed to Father Sandy and spoke softly. The pastor felt that the Japanese was friendly and that his message was a kind one, but he had no idea what he was saying. Then, even softer and as if more afraid than ever, the soldier whispered in halting English: "You flee, not die. Not flee, you die."

Father Sandy, completely oblivious of the message itself, thanked the colonel over and over for his kindness performed at such risk to himself. The Japanese went through his little formula again: "You flee, not die. Not flee, you die," in a kind of panic brought on by his fear that the smiling priest did not understand him. As if for insurance, the colonel went all over it again in Japanese, even raising his voice, as people unconsciously do in their attempt to make one who does not understand their language, somehow understand it after all.

Once more the English version, and then the Japanese scurried down the hill toward the beach. Father Sandy watched him until he disappeared around the hill. Then he went over to the church and knelt down. He remained kneeling a long time—an hour, maybe two. When he got up and went out and walked over to his rectory he was not smiling, but anyone could tell he was happy and at great peace.

Knowing that mail could be smuggled off the island, even though there was no way to get an answer back from the mainland, Father Sandy sat down and wrote to Father Lavin. It was not a long letter; not even a letter at all. Just a note. And the heart of the message was one sentence, fifteen words long:

"It is my duty to stay at Sancian with the people and administer the Sacraments."

When that sentence had been written, the fifteen words made but one—a word that roared with screaming speed around the world and up to heaven—"Victory."

Father Sandy had not long to wait. Just three days.

Enough time to have some dreams, to finish the memories, to say some prayers, to fan to white heat the final dedication.

Early on the morning of December 16, 1941, a motorboat with three Japanese soldiers and one civilian pulled up on the beach at Sancian Island. The four men got out of the boat, walked up to the mission, and ordered Father Sandy to follow them. Back to the boat they marched Father Sandy between his captors. One of Father Sandy's catechists—Ching Wan Naam—came running after them. Ching asked permission to be with Father Sandy, to go with him wherever he went. It was granted, as he asked.

The three Japanese soldiers and their one civilian companion, Ching and Father Sandy, boarded the boat. The motor was started, and the boat pulled away from shore.

That much is known from the Catholics who saw it. . . . Out in deep water the three Japanese soldiers and their civilian companion put Father Sandy in a pig basket and dropped him into the sea.

That much we know from the civilian who did it. . . . "The good shepherd giveth his life for his sheep" . . . "He that loses his life for My sake, shall find it. . . ."

That much we know—from Christ Who said it.

EPILOGUE : **to lead the way**

There remains only a word to be said about the present ferocious persecution of the Church in China—and of Father Cairns' place in it.

In 1949, after twenty-seven years of sustained effort to overthrow the government of the Republic of China, Mao Tse-tung and his Communist comrades marched into Peiping—conquerors and masters of all the regions of China. The Red Armies had swept down through the twenty-six provinces of the nation, establishing everywhere the slave rule that has brought an ancient, proud, and noble race to ruin. In no previous revolution, war, or human holocaust, either in the days of Attila or in the time of Stalin, have so many people been slaughtered in so short a period. The Church, recognized by Mao as the threat it is to any regime of slavery and savagery, came early under attack in the Red reign of terror. The churches were closed. Religious services were banned. Catholic schools were taken over by the State. Catholic orphanages were emptied and converted into military barracks. Foreign missionary bishops, priests, Brothers, and Sisters were herded into jails and prisons wholesale for eventual execution or deportation. The Chinese clergy was decimated, and more than half of the remaining native priests are at this time serving prison terms or dying in slave labor gangs. The laity, both in the cities and in the country districts, are now cajoled and beaten in turn to give up the Faith. As a consummating tactic of deviltry, the Communists have established a schismatic "Catholic" Church to confuse a people so long deprived of Sacrifice and Sacrament.

Francis X. Ford, the Maryknoll martyr and bishop from Brooklyn, lies in a prisoner's grave in Canton, a victim of the Red frenzy to stamp out everything Godlike.

The Canadian Nuns were arrested and tried and sentenced for "killing" orphans.

The Bishop of Shanghai and twenty-three of his priests and some two hundred of his flock are in jail being tortured for spreading "anti-communist" propaganda.

Over 5000 foreign missioners have been deported or executed after long months in prison since Mao Tse-tung took the butcher knife to the Mystical Body of Christ in China.

But the Faith grows stronger in China at each day's new desecration.

The Catholic people tell their beads and baptize their babies behind the locked doors of midnight.

The glorious saga of the loyalty and heroism of the Chinese clergy who continue to feed the sheep from holes of hiding until they are caught and killed, will be repeated by Catholics the world over until the end of time.

The Chinese Sisters, who in the face of daily danger of death, go about their work of feeding the poor, nursing the sick, mothering orphans, are among the noblest women who have ever walked this earth since Mary of Nazareth's assumption into heaven.

How long will all this fiendishness and slaughter last? How much more can the Chinese endure?

The Church is undergoing her passion in China. The final crucifixion approaches. Then comes the glory and victory of her Easter.

Father Sandy's place in this Holy Week of the nation is to lead the shepherds and the sheep of China along the way he trod. He went first to lead the way, to blaze the trail, to roll away the stone. And when the sea of today's martyrs' blood has watered down the final inch of Chinese soil, and the seed of conversion has blossomed in 450 million Chinese hearts, then the name of Robert John Cairns, Maryknoll Missioner and Martyr, will be blessed forever by the people whom he loved and died for.

APPENDIX : **Holy Cross College and St. Mary's Seminary in Bobby Cairns' day**

When Bobby Cairns entered Holy Cross, it ranked as a small college of about 400 students. When he graduated, it still ranked as a small college of 547 students. But its Catholic scholarship and New England erudition had raised it to prominence among the colleges of the East.

At the time of Bobby's arrival at the college, its president was Father Thomas E. Murphy, S.J.; when he left it, Father Joseph N. Dinand, S.J., future Vicar Apostolic of Jamaica, held that office. No faculty of the Holy Cross size boasted more distinguished names; even two generations later, many of them evoke memories among thousands of alumni, not only of Holy Cross, but of other colleges, also.

Those distinguished names include the following: Fathers John F. Lehy, Ferdinand A. Rousseau, Edmund J. Burke, James A. Mullen, Thomas F. McLoughlin, Robert Schwickerath, Michael J. Mahony, Thomas B. Chestwood, Owen A. Hill, George L. Coyle, John F. X. Pyne, Daniel

P. Crowley, Peter Schweitzer, Michael Earls, John V. Coveney, John W. Wheeler, Francis J. McNiff, Louis Weber, John J. Fleming, Frederick B. Heaney, Edward T. Farrell; also the then scholastics, Charles L. Kimball, Gerald C. Treacy, George H. Derry, Henry F. Wessling, David C. Cronin, Timothy F. Scanlan, Charles F. Connors, Henry M. Borck.

The Class of 1914, of which the energetic Robert E. Ferry, later widely known in the publishing field, was president, is one of the famous classes of Holy Cross, and none contributed more to its fame than the gregarious Bobby Cairns. And none knew the faculty and student body better than he. During his years at prep school and college, four future bishops were students, and Bobby was able to include them in his comprehensive list of friends. Three were seniors to him: the late Bishop William J. Hafey, '09, of Scranton; Bishop John P. Treacy, '12, of La Crosse; and the late Auxiliary Bishop Thomas F. Markham, '13, of Boston. One was his junior: Coadjutor Bishop Daniel J. Feeney, '17, of Portland. None was senior to him in age, and none junior in youthful spirit.

Despite the obligation of self-support that Bobby Cairns had assumed, there was no man in the college busier in extra-curricular activities. Even then, Holy Cross had attained fame in athletics as well as in scholarship. Men like Bill Carrigan, manager of the Boston Red Sox, and Jack Barry, Pete Noonan, and Andy Coakley of the Philadelphia Athletics had gone from Mount St. James to major league baseball. Bobby Cairns, because of poor eyesight, could not excel in athletics, although he played an excellent game of tennis. But he had a talent for music, and he used that for the honor of Holy Cross.

Bobby had learned to play the mandolin when quite young, and throughout his life he never entirely neglected

"Mandy." As a prose writer and as a poet, he not only became editor-in-chief of *The Purple,* but also turned out college songs—some of them in Scotch dialect. His "Ficht, Holy Cross!" which became popular with the orchestras and in the theaters of the region, made its debut at a baseball game with Dartmouth College. The Dartmouth boys were intrigued by it, but could not quite understand it. It was English, and yet, in a way, it wasn't. They were so diverted, trying to make out the wording, that their attention was distracted from the game, and disastrous figures appeared on their score. Walter McManus, pitching for Holy Cross, got the credit for the victory, but he would have been willing to give the song writer a major share in the credit. Bobby had not only written the words for the song; he had also composed the music, with the help of his friend, Will Hardy.

For extracurricular activity, Bobby shone brilliantly in his dual capacity of editor and business manager of *The Purple Patcher,* the senior yearbook. If the income tax had been in effect and if the *Patcher* had not been a non-profit project, Bobby would most certainly have placed it in a high tax bracket. The Worcester dailies were no doubt delighted when this Holy Cross competitor for a share in the advertising dollars of Worcester corporations and partnerships, retired eventually from that field.

To multitudinous other activities, Bobby added in his sophomore year the managing of the campaign of his sister, Miss Janet A. Cairns, in the Worcester *Daily Telegram's* "Around the World" contest. The winners were decided by ballot. Of course, with Bobby spearheading her campaign, Janet Cairns easily became one of the three winners.

Memorable as were Bobby's achievements for *The Purple* in the business field, he was best remembered at Holy Cross as editor. *The Purple* had always ranked high among college literary magazines, and Bobby's prose, sparked by his enthusiasm and fed by his experience and imagination, more than measured up to the standard. But his poetry, especially that in Scotch dialect, greatly enhanced *The Purple's* prestige. There were few issues, in his time at the college, not graced by his verses. "Whist, Gang Tae Sleep" received from a contemporary publication commendation for being "as simple and unaffected as a song by Burns—as Scotch as the heather itself."

Whist, Gang Tae Sleep.

> Ha, birdie, wee, wee wain,
> Gang tae sleep noo, close yer 'ee,
> My bonnie babe sae braw an' fain,
> Shair yere a' the warld tae me.
> Yer faither's gane awa' tae toon
> Markin' fer oor claes an' shoon,
> My sonsie bairn, he'll shin return
> O'er brae an' dyke an' ilka burn.

> Ha, birdie, wee, wee wain,
> Gang tae sleep noo, close yer 'ee,
> My bonnie babe sae braw an' fain,
> Shair yere a' the warld tae me.
> I swing ye, bairnie, neist my heart,
> 'Twud break in twa frae you tae part.
> Whist ye, chiel, noo sleep again,
> Ha, birdie, wee, wee wain.

Bobby Cairns registered as a day scholar at Holy Cross, and lived at home with his mother and the rest of his family. He escorted his sisters to football games, dances, and other entertainments, striving to be equally attentive to all. His parents' ten-room home on Dix Street turned out to be hardly less a center for Holy Cross activity than the college itself. When Bobby telephoned his mother to say that he would be bringing home some friends, she never knew whether to expect two or ten. After dinner the Cairns orchestra would provide music: Marion or Minnie at the piano, George with his violin, Bobby with the mandolin. The guests and the other members of the family would contribute favorite songs, while Mrs. Cairns—"Katy the Cook" as Bobby called her—presided benignly. On occasion, young Archie, instead of singing, would add to the gaiety by howling along with Beauty, the dog.

At least once, following a Holy Cross dance, Bobby invited so many friends to spend the night with his family that the ten-room house could not accommodate all, and a few were compelled to retire to the barn for the night, taking their formal attire with them. Always the impressario with a full program planned, Bobby would be likely to rout guests out at five o'clock in the morning, for a game of tennis.

"Plan twelve things a day, and you may get six done; plan six, and you may do three," was his rule of action, then and until the end of his life.

Of the 172 students who had entered Holy Cross College as the Class of 1914, or who had later become affiliated with it, ninety-five received degrees on Commencement Terrace, June 14, 1914, in the presence of Bishop Thomas D. Beaven of Springfield and of the Governor of Massachusetts. The presence of the Commonwealth's chief Executive had become a Holy Cross tradition. The Commencement orations reflected the temper of those presumably peaceful times, on the eve of World War I.

Joseph S. Dineen, now a distinguished Jesuit, formerly rector of St. Joseph's College in Philadelphia and of the Jesuit novitiate in Wernersville, discussed "The Moral Aspects of Modern Times." The late Walter J. Hutchinson, who became a noted motion-picture executive, spoke on

"Evolution and Faith." The late Francis D. Comerford, who was to become president of the New England Power Company and also president of the Boston Edison Company, had chosen "International Arbitration" for his subject. The future Monsignor William F. Kearny, now a Bridgeport, Connecticut, pastor, directed his remarks to "Ideals in Collegiate Training."

St. Mary's Seminary was, without doubt, the most famous theological school in the United States. It had trained more priests, and listed more bishops among its alumni, than any other seminary. Its history developed coextensively with that of the hierarchy in the United States, the seminary having been first established in 1791 by four Sulpician Fathers driven from France by the Revolution there. John Carroll, the nation's first Catholic bishop, had been consecrated but a year before St. Mary's Seminary was founded. That was two years after the adoption of the Bill of Rights, and George Washington was then in the second year of his first term as President of the United States.

When the Sulpicians established St. Mary's, the original building, formerly a tavern, was situated on the outskirts of Baltimore. When Bobby arrived as a student, the city surrounded the site, thus eventually making necessary the erection of the present magnificent structure in suburban Roland Park. But the old, Paca Street seminary served during Bobby's two years there and for many years afterward; and it is now the minor seminary.

St. Mary's is rich in Catholic and American tradition. Seven other great American seminaries or colleges were subsequently founded by Sulpicians from St. Mary's halls: Mount St. Mary's, Emmitsburg, Maryland; St. Charles College, Ellicot City, Maryland; St. John's Seminary, Brighton, Massachusetts; St. Joseph's Seminary, Yonkers,

New York; St. Patrick's Seminary, Menlo Park, California; the Sulpician College at the Catholic University of America; St. Edward's Seminary near Seattle, Washington; and one formerly conducted in Kentucky.

A "Who's Who" of alumni from St. Mary's would be almost an outline of the Catholic Church in the United States, and of scores of its dioceses. The Third Plenary Council of Baltimore (during which Mary Immaculate was officially chosen as the Patroness of America) and other important ecclesiastical conferences, have been held there. St. Mary's archives are among the richest sources of Catholic America's Church history. After a century and a quarter of service to the Church and to the nation, St. Mary's close connection with the past was indicated by the fact that, in 1914, the seminary was under the direction of only its sixth superior, the beloved Father Edward Randall Dyer.

St. Mary's introduced Bobby to a priestly and spiritual atmosphere that influenced him forever. There was a touch of Holy Cross about St. Mary's, too, for Bobby's classmates included several youths who had been graduated with him in the previous June. Those future priests were: Clarence H. Coughlan, from Maine; Michael E. Kearney and William F. Kearney, from Connecticut; Bernard A. Kerrigan and Jeremiah C. Murphy, from Massachusetts. Other Holy Cross graduates—including John P. Donahue, Eugene F. Marshall, Joseph M. Ryan, Richard J. Dee, John P. Shannon, Jeremiah J. McCarthy, John D. Monahan, and Thomas A. Boland—had gone to the Sulpician Seminary in Montreal, Canada. John D. McGowan went to the archdiocese of New York, where he is now, as a member of the Papal Household, pastor at Rye.

Bobby's class at St. Mary's proved to be an unusual one. Among the thirty-three members who went on to the priesthood, were the future Bishop Thomas K. Gorman of Reno, now ordinary of Dallas and Fort Worth, and eight future monsignori. The latter included the following students: William F. Kearney, of Bridgeport, Connecticut; John J. Laffey, of Mooseheart, Illinois; Luigi A. Ligutti, of Des Moines, Iowa (now the noted leader of the Catholic Rural Life Conference); William J. Meredith, of the diocese of Richmond, Virginia; Joseph P. Morrison, of the archdiocese of Chicago; Harry A. Quinn and John F. Leary, of the archdiocese of Baltimore; E. Jerome Winter, of the archdiocese of Washington. Eugene F. Marshall and John P. Donahue, two of Bobby's closest friends at Holy Cross, are also members of the Papal Household, and priests of the diocese of Springfield, Massachusetts.

Father Louis A. Arand, of the same class, joined the Sulpicians; Father Anthony J. Paulus, like Bobby, went to the Maryknollers; Father Sylvester T. Healy became a Benedictine. Other classmates and their present locations are as follows: Fathers George E. Archambault and the late Charles C. Curran, of Rhode Island; John Cash, Leo A. Kerrigan, Melvin A. Melville, and Wenceslaus Panek, of Iowa; Felix S. Childs, George B. Healy, and Armand J. Levasseur, of Massachusetts; Cornelius Enright and Peter Pojnar, of Maine; Joseph L. Curran and William A. Nelligan, of Maryland; Thomas J. Mackin, of Chicago, distinguished as a missioner in South Carolina; Thomas F. Millet, of California; Paul I. Sikora, of West Virginia; John K. Sharp, the noted historian of the diocese of Brooklyn. Another fellow student and close friend, Father Edward F. Murphy, joined the Josephite Fathers and attained fame as an author and as a missioner among Negroes.

Father Edward A. Cerny, S.S., now of the faculty at St. Mary's, became one of Bobby's close friends at the seminary, although two years ahead of him in class. Father Cerny remembers that Bobby found the transition from college to seminary somewhat difficult. At Holy Cross, innumerable outside activities had consumed the surplus energy of Bobby as student and as man of affairs. Moreover, his mind never had been given to speculation, and he had never been a bookish man. Yet given a concrete situation, he could always size it up rapidly and with clarity.

Ten years after entering St. Mary's, memories of the seminary lingered refreshingly in Father Sandy's mind. Writing to the editor of *The Voice,* the student publication at St. Mary's, he said: "In China, although we are separated from you by many a mile, we hear *The Voice,* and listen intently to all it has to say. Again I see myself with the St. Camillus' men (Apostles of the Sick) at Bay View, or at 'the Pen' or some Sunday school; I walk once more on the roof; I try my hand at tennis or baseball or handball in the yard; and I go up the steps and into the chapel, the drawing of which you have worked into the title of your paper."

The memories of Holy Cross and St. Mary's, we can easily believe, filled many of the lonely hours Father Sandy spent on the missions. To his friends and companions of his student days his mind turned often after he was separated from them. For all the miles and miles of land and sea that kept them from him, they were still part of him, part of the happy, memorable smile of Father Sandy.

selections from
Father Cairns' writings

The unpretentious jottings of Father "Sandy" reveal first of all his dedication to the cause of the missions, and then his warmth and generosity, his enduring optimism and heroic grit. His irre-pressible humor reaches across oceans because it so frequently skirts pathos. And occasionally the simple strength of Father "Sandy's" love of God gives wings to his words, so that they leave with us a rare glimpse of remembered beauty.

Father Cairns did not think of himself as a gifted writer. The letters and articles he penned—often on crowded trains, busses and junks—were written out of a sense of responsibility to his mission calling. The great missionary movement of the United States that marked the twentieth-century history of the Church was just beginning. The writings of the missioners were aimed at feeding the newly lighted flame of charity that was glowing in the hearts of Americans.

CONTENTS

FROM A SANDY SOIL

Och Faith'r Superior dear,
I'm guy weel here,
   An' feelin' fine an' dandy
Frae lang syne awa
Here's a page or twa
   Frae yer wee red-bearded SANDY.

The *Cabbages and Kings* quoted by O. Henry are not more of a contrast to each other than the *Tiger Bones* and *Mandarins* in Yeungkong.

The mandarin is the boss of the town; but the name on paper is more exalted than the reality in the flesh. For though the title is dignified and highly respected in some large centers, yet it is not always so in the smaller places. In fact, since the Republic's birth in 1911, the word mandarin often means what an American would call a clever politician or what a Chinese country dweller might term a bandit-leader. For in these troublesome times, when the innocent suffering villages cannot tell who is who, mandarins come and go, sometimes more frequently than the seasons. He's "here today and gone tomorrow"; "survival of the fittest"—provided he is fitted with a "pull" with the political Sun or leader. Or it may be "push" with guns and ammunition which made him "what he is today"—a mandarin.

In the room below me, we had a couple of dignitaries sitting at our rice table recently. I was surprised to learn that they were the two local mandarins, civil and military, and I had the old exalted idea of them—that I should learn words of wisdom from the great high mandarins.

Both were in charge of the defense of Yeungkong during the siege of our city. Siege is not a very good word for it was only a slight siege with sham battles. The bandits, for several days, shot occasional bullets at the city wall. Yeungkong soldiers within the wall, returned the fire with one single cannon, a rapid-fire gun or two, and a couple of hundred rifles. Finally the mandarins and all the local soldiers evacuated the city and left it to the oncoming bandit plunderers, who robbed and pillaged to their hearts' content. No one was charged with "breaking and entering," for there are no police, and the bandits were the only representatives of government and justice. These fellows, after stealing the valuables of the city, set up their own mandarin, to whom the suffering Yeungkong people could not very well appeal for justice.

In the six months I've been in Yeungkong, there have been almost that many mandarins. It is an exalted term, but as Mr. Goldberg says: "It doesn't mean anything"; so tell Political Jim of Ward Three not to come over here to aspire to a mandarincy. Do you think that the Jesse James type of mandarin is beloved by the people? He is—not. The Chinese country folk love him about as much as they do a wild tiger. They would like him much better if he were dead.

TIGER BONES ELIXIR

However, the Chinese *do* have some regard for real tigers, provided they are lifeless. Ho Sin Shaang, the venerable catechist, when on a trip through the missions, invested twenty dollars in a dead tiger. It was killed near Chiklung— do not get alarmed, though; we haven't seen one running in our chapel, and we don't expect to see one alive because they are rare specimens.

Today, the veranda in front of my door was a scene of activity, for the tiger bones were being canned. The house-boys wiped each bone and placed it carefully in a large jar now sealed hermetically. The boy who was the victim of my *Beginners' Course in Chinese* says that for *ng nin* these bones will be preserved in a special liquid, and at the end of that five years he will "drink-eat" the stuff. He claims it will cure him of all the ills that flesh is heir to. But I'm Sandy, "I hae me doots."

TRIALS OF A HEAVYWEIGHT

Early in the morning, I was assured of a bamboo chair with a couple of bearers to carry me northward to Kochow, for I had to go to confession and needed some advice, particularly about the new school. But the chair bearers did not arrive. "You will surely get a bamboo chair after three *po lo,*" said my teacher, "there are always 'carry nobility' to be had at that place."

So about 10:30 we ferried across the Fachow River and began our walk. At the end of the three *po lo,* which is thirty Chinese miles, or about ten American miles, we stopped and opened our *Baltimore Review* to eat the lunch we had carried along wrapped in the good old Catholic paper. The meal consisted of bread, eggs, and a piece of cake; supplemented by the wayside inn's Chinese sweet potatoes and hot ricewater, which served as tea.

The hunger of Chinese hens and chickens was brought home forcibly, when they quarreled among themselves for the eggshells which dropped to the ground as I dined. I was surrounded by brown hens and chickens, black dogs and yellow men, all watching me intently.

Lunch took fifteen minutes, and we were on our way again, at a pretty good gait, and I wish you could have seen me in a white suit, amber eyeglasses, and a five-year-old black fedora; while the whole Sandy was covered with a black umbrella, open to the full, to protect me and my head from the glaring sun. I wore my beads—as usual when walking—perspiration beads, which trickled down my forehead and across the lens of my glasses, causing an optical delusion, which changed the contour of the narrow path.

The three *po lo,* or ten U.S. miles, were covered by this

time, but not a chair could be found, though my inquiry was diligent. After covering about five *po lo,* (over fifteen U.S. miles) my joy was supreme, for we met two bearers with an empty chair; but the joy soon changed into sorrow, for they gave my heavy profile the "once over" and quickly said *"mo lik."* They meant, " 'We have no strength,' at least not enough to carry such a heavyweight as you." And if they only knew—I had already lost several pounds since leaving Fachow in the morning.

Constantly till three-thirty we walked, and I in the meantime tried to recite the Divine Office, though I fear that I was somewhat lax in the rubric which requires the priest to say his office *"pie, attente et devote."*

Ten minutes were required for our afternoon tea. The bowl in which the rice was served me was not too clean, the chopsticks were handed me from a jar on the table, and the cook passed them to me according to the Chinese custom at roadside inns. That is, the ends of the "quick baby," *faai tsz* (as the Chinese term the chopsticks), which were soon to pass my lips, were first pawed over by the soiled hands of our genial host, Mr. Cook.

Four bowls of hot ricewater, and one of rice gave me the strength to push onward, after wasting ten minutes at this Chinese restaurant. Danger of not arriving at Kochow before dark, made me attempt to buy a lantern or torch, but there were none to be purchased.

The innkeeper sold food, he said, not lamps, lanterns or torches. "But we won't be able to see the road," objected Sandy. "Oh, yes you will," he answered, "you can easily arrive before you need a light." (I found out afterwards, though, that this was merely his polite way of refusing to sell. Would your Maryknoll philosophers class this under Mental Reservation?)

122

CHINESE ROADS ARE DIFFERENT

So we added to our speed. I had thought before that I was
going at top-notch, but now we "stepped on the gas and de-
fied the speed officers"—they couldn't see us through the
dust we raised. And for the fun and excitement of the thing,
we ran at a dog's trot for a few miles. But it was no use, we
couldn't beat the sun, for his bedtime story was soon broad-
casted, and he retired to peaceful slumber, "and left the
world to darkness and to me."

Then there was nothing to do but keep on going. A
Tsat (Name Seven), a green coolie, whom I was bringing to
Kochow to learn a little gardening, was in the lead; he
refused to let me get at my bag to change my amber sun-
glasses. I wanted the clear white, to avoid the eyestrain;
"It's only a little ways now," said Seven, so I took his word
for it and moved along.

Have you ever had the experience of guiding a car
through a strange, sandy road on a pitch-black night? If
so, recall the strain upon your eyes. Now picture that your
headlights refuse to function, and you have a fair idea of
my predicament.

Chinese roads are not roads, they are walks; narrow,
winding, pathways, often between ricefields, frequently uneven, and nearly always difficult to travel. In order to continue my journey, I was obliged to keep close behind
Seven, and sometimes steadied myself by catching hold of
the bamboo pole slung across his shoulder. As it gradually
became darker, I changed to the lock step such as the Sing
Sing men are said to use—and I watched my guide's feet
as best I could.

Oh boy, Oh boy,
What glee and joy!

> The bright moonbeams,
> My fears alloy.

The yellow beams from the moon's last quarter on a sudden gave me, without expense, a lantern better than any I could buy. But within a half hour, even this lantern went out; for every cloud has a silver lining, but the silver, like the moon, is sometimes hidden.

So we continued on our forward march, though the progress now became very slow. But I sang to myself a favorite ditty of mine:

> "There is somebody waiting for me,
> In a place where I wish I could be,
> With a smile and a wee cup o' tea,
> There is somebody waiting for me."

Farther and farther we walked, nearer and nearer we came to our destination, and to vary the sound of my own voice, I hummed:

> "In Kochow's Maryknoll I'll soon be,
> Paschy, Fred and Bill, I will see
> With a smile and a wee cup o' tea,
> For there's somebody waiting for me."

As we walked along the river's edge toward the terminus of our journey, the real fun began. For the path was covered with small gullies made by the rise and fall of the river; stones were lying across the road, and we were actually forced to pick our way along. I had to grope behind faithful Seven, with my umbrella as a cane, tapping the uneven earth as a blind man does, and feeling with my foot before I completed each step.

We came through a village where a dragon procession

was led by two bright, flaming torches, one of which I would have paid anything for; but I did not dare to ask any of the two score men following the monstrous paper beast. I did try to purchase a Chinese lantern in the village, with the same lack of success as before.

Well, we came finally to Kochow and I was happy. The blisters on my feet were painful, and I was glad that it was dark, for the passers-by could not see that I was limping. But again the happiness was changed—Seven said the mission was two *lay* (Chinese miles) outside the city.

"Hopes springs eternal in the human breast," indeed it does. So I said my Rosary again, and limped along, helped by my umbrella-cane; and I was thankful for the lights in the streets of the city.

The mission doors were closed; I was no longer expected as the knowing Chinese had told the Fathers that it was impossible for me to come now, because I couldn't see the road. I had arrived—so the doors were opened, and a short Sandy Priest with perspiration on his forehead and on his soiled hands, and his whole figure looking the worse for wear, gained entrance into the house, and received an even better welcome than he had anticipated.

Fathers Fitzgerald and Fletcher took the tired traveler in charge, had a good supper made ready, watched their hungry Maryknoller eat, and listened to his recital of how quickly he had covered the nine *po lo,* thirty miles.

After supper the one thing in the whole mission compound that interested me most, was my bed. And I was soon fast asleep.

REDS SEIZE FACHOW

Our school hasn't opened yet. That is lucky, because all the Fachow schools which opened last month have had to close on account of the wars.

On the 7th of this month, 4,000 soldiers on the payroll of the Canton Bolsheviks took Fachow, after several days of fighting. We had a splendid view of the battle, staged on the hill to the south of the city wall. The "Bolschys" kept up firing on the city for days, and nights, too. Sundown doesn't stop the noise of battle around this part of China. At 10 o'clock at night we heard a terrific volley, we were awakened about 2 A.M. by another, and each morning just before dawn the din was terrible.

The poor people were much frightened and with good reason. For no matter who wins, they are always the sufferers. They usually have to supply bed and board for the soldiers, who demand and get whatever they need. At the start the people packed up what few valuables and movable goods they had; and the streets were full of coolies with poles on their shoulders, carrying the baskets to interior villages and safety. Ferry boats stopped running. The coolies burdened with their packs waded across the river waist-deep in water, together with their employers and the latters' families. Houses and shops were securely boarded up, and after a few hours the city was as dead as a doornail.

The mandarin and all the high officials fled, but "Mandy" had the foresight to deposit some of his property at the Catholic mission before he left. Refugees came into our compound; the men lived in the outbuildings, and the women occupied the first floor of the house. We removed the Blessed Sacrament, and spent the days dodging bullets.

Finally the city yielded. The local soldiers escaped to Shekshing 35 miles south of Fachow, and left our walled city in the hands of the Bolsheviks.

BULLET-DODGING DAYS

About the 17th, however, the pastor's friend, General Chan Choh Ying, commanding those who had retreated from Fachow, returned with 3,000 reinforcements, machine guns and cannon, to retake the city. He meant business, too, if one can judge by the way he went about it. But the Bolsheviks sent to Kochow for more soldiers, and in three days Chan Choh Ying and our old home guard had to beat a retreat.

Bullets whistled around our heads in great numbers. One which we have kept as a souvenir crashed through a window frame, broke a hole in the wall, knocked the plaster out, and then fell harmlessly on the desk. One of us was only a few feet from the spot, so you may well believe we went downstairs in a hurry.

On the 25th, there was a young revolution in the Fachow Reds' camp, when nearly 1,000 soldiers refused to obey orders. I never saw a town shut up so quickly. Again the ferrymen anchored their boats, hundreds of people waded across the river, coolies carried their poles with heavy baggage on either end and all was excitement. The boards were put up in the front of houses and shops, business stopped, and the streets were deserted. The rebels were marched out upon the beach in front of the mission. They were disarmed, their guns were stacked up, the ammunition was put in piles, and we expected that they would be shot. But no; instead, happily, each man was given two ounces of opium as his pay, and all were sent home. A few hours, and the excitement was over.

We had a happy Thanksgiving because a long-lost box of cookies, jam and candy arrived just in time for the feast day. So we were thankful to Divine Providence for keeping us safe during the joyful bullet-dodging days, and to Father Fletcher's benefactor who helped out when we were living on "war rations."

MANY BEGIN WELL

In Rodriguez's *Christian Perfection*, I came across a quotation which you used to hammer on (I hope you do so yet, for it's worth it) and it is this: "It's easy enough to start things; the real test is in keeping them up—completing them." Or in the words of St. Jerome, "It is no matter to begin, but the chief thing is to perfect what we have begun; for it is in that alone that perfection consists." In another place he says, "Many begin well, but few end well."

This idea certainly applies to our work in China, where perseverance is necessary if we would accomplish anything in the spiritual line for ourselves and for others.

Again, you often quoted, "A man's ideals in the seminary are the highest he will ever reach . . . he cannot get beyond them; so aim high." Here on the mission, our wills are no stronger in keeping our resolutions, no stronger in fighting sin, no stronger in keeping at the language books when other easier and pleasanter things call us—our wills are no stronger than we have developed them in the seminary, by aiming at *high* ideals.

And your idea, "It is easy to start things, but the man of God must *keep them up*," has meant so much to me that I hope you will continue to impart it to the seminarians, in season and out of season, for to my mind it is of paramount importance.

AN INQUISITIVE BODY

Belmont is a town of some pretensions, for it has honest-to-goodness brick buildings, including a tall fortified pawnshop, which should rather be called a storage house for valuables during bandits' visits.

And the place seems chock-full of boys who are swarming to get a glimpse of the white-robed foreigner.

Twenty-eight received Holy Communion this morning, and baptism was administered, after Mass, to six—two men, two boys, and two infant girls.

During my thanksgiving after Mass and baptisms, as I knelt before the altar table, someone became interested in my rubber-soled "gym" shoes, which I find good for walking. I tried not to notice the inquisitive inspector when he raised my cassock to better examine the white shoes. I made never a move even when the inquisitive body lifted my ankle, as a blacksmith does when he is shoeing a horse, though I must confess that I was tempted to say and do something.

When my Breviary was attended to, I continued taking the census of the parish. The town boys, Catholics and pagans, have been following me every time I went out; so I gave them a good walk all round and through Belmont. Afterwards I gained their good will by teaching them to play "Three O'Cat." When we returned to the chapel, I gave the little heathens a talk about the true God.

Tonight I booked eight boys for the new Fachow school, so this will be a Catholic nucleus for our Holy Cross School which had only pagan pupils enrolled before these were added.

I am picking up a few words of Chinese and am being helped by associating so intimately with the people.

A SCHOOL STRIKE

On Confucius' birthday, all the schools paraded through town and our drums and bugles were borrowed to lead the torchlight procession. Ingenious shaped lanterns were made by the schoolboys—dragons, clocks, books, balls, all interiorly lighted with candles, lamps, or flashlights. These bright lanterns made the parade attractive to watch, though the din of drums, bugles, and tom-toms was deafening.

Three separate schools had dragons with huge paper heads and flashlights for eyes. Under each head walked two men, one to support it, and the other to move it from one side of the street to the other. The paper body was supported by about twenty boys who moved from side to side like a writhing serpent. The dragons represented much work and great expense on the part of the schoolboys who fashioned them.

It looked to me like a religious superstition, but my Catholic professors assure me that it is not. Confucius is to the Chinese mind the patron of education and is revered as such by nearly all students in China.

''TEN PARTS GOOD''

The distribution of prizes brought many visitors to Holy Cross School. The mandarin added to the splendor of the occasion, for he gave the prizes to the boys.

On Monday, invitations carefully written on red paper, were inserted in their red envelopes and sent by messengers to the best men about town. On Wednesday, invitation number two was dispatched with the same profusion of colored stationery. Invitation number three was given by the Father personally on Thursday.

The social scale has its gradations. Many people received the first letter; a few important men received the second; but the third personal invitation was extended only to the mandarin, Board of Education, a lawyer, and the school principals.

At one o'clock, on Friday, the affair began, with the pastor in the limelight, facing the mandarin, officials of the Board of Education, superintendents of all the Fachow schools, other business and professional men, and the fathers of several of the boys. In the back of the pagan temple (our temporary school), the students with clean white suits and new hair cuts were all expectancy.

Leung Sin Shaang, Holy Cross School's secretary, began the exercises by reading in Chinese from a large paper pasted on the wall. After each paragraph, he bowed first to the pastor, then to the audience, which stood during the reading, and then three times to the *Shen Fu* (priest), who had to return the triple bow (my back was almost broken).

Each school principal in real brotherly spirit read from a paper, upon which was written his speech of welcome to the new school, Holy Cross. Our head teacher, Chan Sin Shaang, responded to these speeches and the *Shen Fu* said a few words.

Dinner was served in Chinese style in the school. Then the whole crowd came to the chapel where they approved the glaring colors on our new Chinese altar—"ten parts good," they murmured, which is superlative commendation. Next, all crowded into our dining room to listen to the *kay hay* as they call the phonograph. Everything in the room was minutely examined, and the price of each piece of furniture had to be told to the human "question boxes."

Discipline is so strange to the schoolboys that it would need a couple of husky traffic officers to enforce it properly. One day recently, the whole school skipped an hour of class, and I kept the boys a half hour after school—a punishment unheard of by the easygoing Chinese lads. The next day, they showed their resentment by staying away from doctrine class, and when I threatened to penalize them with more study to make up for it, the whole school, with the exception of two Catholic boys, went on a strike. The strikers hung round the school yard from twelve until three, when I delivered the ultimatum, "Come to class or you cannot eat or sleep at Holy Cross School." They refused and had to dine and spend the night round town wherever they could.

In the morning they returned. I unlocked the school and said that all who wished could get their belongings and leave; but not a single boy went home, and the strike was broken.

I heard that six of the day scholars received a beating from their fathers for skipping class and refusing to study, which augurs well for the future of young China.

But the school strike has shown me that we need more patience if we would deal effectively with the Chinese who are so different from ourselves.

THE SUNCHONG DISPENSARY

The dispensary is one of the cheeriest rooms in the house; white and sanitary. With its cabinets of instruments and medicines, it gives evidence of having equipment to cure the ills that flesh is heir to.

And it is very popular, even though it has not been in operation very long. Cuts and bruises, aches and sprains, everything *frae a wee cut tae a meenor operation* gets relief here at the hands of the Father. He has already won his way into the hearts of several Chinese, and his fame as a "Doctor" is spreading. For though he tells them that he is not a doctor, but a priest, their "spiritual father," yet he does them so much good that they continue to call him "Doc."

CASES TREATED

Here are some of the cases treated recently: Our cook was the first patient, with his infected hand which had to be lanced; next, the houseboy's chronic tonsillitis. Then Fr. Sheridan arrived with malaria, an intermittent fever of one hundred and six degrees, off and on, for six days, when he returned to normal under the quinine treatment. Finally the cook suddenly got a spasm of the stomach with convulsions, but, in a few hours, he was well again.

But charity that is the right kind, though it may start at home, does not remain there. So when a Catholic eight-year-old boy accidentally fell from a bridge into the empty river-bed at low tide, and, landing in the mud, ran a sharp piece of bamboo through the upper left eyelid and received several scalp wounds, the mission dispensary, just around the corner, immediately came to mind. First aid was administered, and, the following morning (as the doctor in town could not be reached), three stitches were taken in the eyelid by the attending "surgeon," assisted by Brother Michael, who happened to be visiting here. When the last dressing was removed the eyesight not only was not lost, but was completely normal. A fraction of an inch lower, and the youngster would have been blind in one eye the rest of his life.

THE WAY OF KINDNESS

But he was a Christian. *Other sheep I have* . . . , and it is especially to the "other sheep" that we have been sent; so we were more than grateful for the publicity received by the toddling youngster, swathed in snowy bandages for a month, going out daily from the mission dispensary.

We soon welcomed our first pagan, brought in by the happy mother of the healed boy. The new patient's trouble was in the index finger of his left hand, the end of which he had partly severed six days before. He went to some Chinese for aid, and received, along with a lot of "goo" smeared on the finger, a nice case of infection, and, later, gangrene. In four days, he left us with a sound finger once more. But, in the meantime, he had brought his mother with a five-day-old dog bite on her ankle, which had become infected.

And so it goes on—an endless chain, which, link by link, draws the mysterious, unknown foreigner, with a foreign message, into the good graces and good will of the people.

Seeds of kindness and little favors first, which water and prepare the soil for the seeds of faith to follow when the planting time comes, when, as St. Paul says, the doors of opportunities are open to us. And thus we work, in a roundabout way, but the surest way, the way of human kindness; slowly, against many odds, but surely, as sure as our Eucharistic Host, our Co-worker, is working with us and in us for the greater honor and glory of His heavenly Father.

We have about three hundred dollars' worth of medicines, instruments, and sanitary furniture on hand, and the man, woman, or child who offers us something to pay for them will cause the wrinkles of worry to fade from our foreheads and will cover our faces with the smile that won't come off.

SLIGHTLY MORE DIFFICULT

In general, there is but little difference between a pastor in the homeland and one in China. Both administer the sacraments and take care of the souls entrusted to them. Each is the spiritual leader and adviser of his people.

However, in the actual performance of duties, there are differences which might well be noted. For example, take the sacraments. Most likely you were baptized in church. In China, the priest often baptizes away from his church in a village, and many of the baptized are grown-ups. This requires a long course of instruction, the engaging of catechists (native teachers of religion), and expensive travel.

For Confession, a priest in China must study a strange language for at least a year. And afterwards, if changed to another locality, he sometimes must study another dialect. He must hear all women's confessions before nightfall. Many people are not well educated or carefully instructed; they do not have opportunities for frequent confessions; consequently, some confessions are not as satisfactory as in America.

A marriage in China often requires the priest's presence the night before, and at a banquet which may mean two or three days' time, lost, strayed, or stolen.

The only difference between your pastor and a pastor in China is the difference of language, customs, and distances. The duties of each pastor are the same, but possibly the proper performance of them in China is slightly more difficult.

A DAMP WELCOME

Yesterday morning, to get a good start, I said Mass at half-past three and left here at daylight. A motor boat brought me to Sunning City: a bus transported me to a place called Sheung Chaak; a bicycle finished the journey to Yuen Taam mission station, where I attended to some business at high noon.

At Yuen Taam, though I expected a good welcome, I was met by a delegation of about fifteen "weeping willows" —women and girls who protested the removal of their beloved Sister Ngan Koo Neung. She had been with them a year. I tried to pacify them as well as I could; I told them of my recent visit to Canton during the Reds' "Reign of Terror"; I thought up some funny stories for them, but nothing could stop the "shower." It was tears, tears, tears —just tiers of tears. I was so tired, finally, that I excused myself from the sob party and went to bed.

After Mass the following morning, the crying began again with renewed vigor, and the good ladies tried to bribe me with some nice cakes and other dainties.

This is a very hard mission station, and one year is long enough for a Sister to stay; besides, Sister Ngan had asked for a change. However, in the face of such evidence of love, she and I had a conference, and she asked to stay with the people another year. When I made the announcement, the rain turned immediately into sunshine. "You have a heart," the good women said. I did not tell them it was Sister Ngan who had the kind heart.

The good Sister should have a vacation, however, so I put her on the boat for Canton, where she can visit her sixty-year-old mother.

MUD-HOUSED PEOPLE

Tso Kong is a poor little village of mud houses with a few brick dwellings for variety's sake. But mud houses can make happy homes. Some of the families are, I dare say, the happiest in the world. Like Sir Galahad they can say: "My strength is as the strength of ten because my heart is pure."

And it is these pure-souled, mud-housed people who realize what our Faith means. They treat the priests and catechists with reverence, devotion, and love. Not satisfied with giving us the *de luxe* room in the best house in the village (which was not so good, but was the best they had), poor as they are, they bought us a house of our own! It's mud-made, floorless, damp, dark, dank—but it's HOME. I slept there last night, and offered Mass on a table near my bed this morning.

The faithful are few, but *very* faithful. I had eight confessions and Communions this morning.

The coming of Jesus Christ upon the altar in that mud-hut a few hours ago was in many respects like His first coming at Bethlehem. Our rough table was crude as the manger, and the few worshippers were like the simple shepherd adorers.

On June 11th, Father Cairns left for Hong Kong by way of Macao, to attend the consecration of Father Valtorta, the new Bishop of Hong Kong. Father Rauschenbach remained at home to direct repairing operations in the chapel, house and school.

The pastor, while at Hong Kong, bought some much needed furniture, after many visits to the auctions where the secondhand articles, "good as new," were secured at prices that met the size of our pocketbook. But the problem was, to get the stuff back to Sunchong. On account of the strict vigilance of the strike pickets, it was impossible to get the goods through Canton; and the strikers had made it so unpleasant for the Macao-Sunchong line, that no boats had run for over a month.

On June 28th, I received definite word from Macao that a boat from Sunchong would leave the next morning. So I hustled about twenty coolies to the boat with the cargo; reached Macao late that night, on account of the low tide; engaged more coolies who worked from midnight until 2:30 in the morning; and finally brought the lighter to a port about two hours from Macao. There all our baggage was packed in the hold of the Sunchong junk.

But it was too good to be true; such connections almost never happen in China. It seems that the Sunchong junk, upon which my baggage was stored, had smuggled three hundred passengers into Macao, past the strike pickets. So the pickets confiscated the boat.

I had to rush out to Cheen Shan and interview the head of the pickets, to save the baggage. He was friendly to me; but we looked rather formidable, when a dozen of these armed bluecoats, and I went together in a small boat to the tabooed junk. I pointed out my baggage, and the strikers gave me permission to take it away. So I hired a large lighter (cargo boat) and returned to Macao with all the baggage; but it almost broke my Scotch heart, for the first lighter had cost me fifty-four dollars. The expenses never seemed to stop.

Brother Michael Hogan was with me, so the delay of nearly a week at Macao, was "nae sae bad." Father Braganca and his assistants at Saint Joseph's Seminary made our stay pleasant. Finally we secured a disreputable sailing vessel, armed to the teeth, and the Captain agreed to take us and our belongings to Sunchong for $110.

So we left Macao the night before the Fourth, at the mystic hour of midnight. I have a suspicion that the boatmen were avoiding the strike pickets, for we were not bothered during our midnight sail out of the harbor.

THE GLORIOUS FOURTH

We had no fireworks, but the Glorious Fourth was not to pass without them. It was pouring rain, when a squall suddenly filled the sails, and water came in at the edge of the junk. Another junk, only a few yards from us, fired about twenty shots—decks were cleared immediately. The Chinese crew and passengers actually *dove* down into the old of the boat, leaving sails and rudder to the mercy of he squall. Eleven loaded cannons, with lighted fuses near by, and seven rifles were on our boat, ready for action; out the attack was so sudden that the men had no time to think of anything but their own safety. I supposed it was a joke until bullets hit the iron armor plate at the side of our junk, then I got under cover in a hurry. There were several bullet holes in our furniture, which was on deck a few feet from where I was standing.

It turned out that the other junk thought we were pirates about to attack them, and we thought that we were being pirated. As a matter of fact both junks were manned by Chinese sailors, trying to make an honest living. But that is pretty hard, for the men on our boat, always on the lookout for pirates, were living in fear and trembling during the entire trip. Several times during the three days, we were all ordered below decks and the crew stood at the cannon and guns, until we passed the pirate-infested waters. Fortunately, we did not meet any pirates, and during our one encounter, none of the men were injured. In any event, the two American passengers spent an exciting Fourth of July.

We were becalmed the second day, with not a breath of wind in our sails. So we paid forty dollars to a passing steamboat to tow us into Sunchong, and thus shortened our happy (?) journey.

A MARYKNOLL PILGRIMAGE TO SANCIAN

Confessions began at 2 P.M., as soon as we left Douglas Wharf in Hong Kong. All priests were given faculties, and temporary confessionals were arranged in several places on the three decks of the boat.

At 2:30 P.M., there was an address by the Rev. D. J. Finn, S.J., of the Regional Seminary, Hong Kong, and Father Finn's subject was: *The Purpose of a Pilgrimage to St. Francis Xavier's Sancian Island.*

At 3:00 P.M., there was congregational singing by the pilgrims, with Rev. Brother Jude Donnelly, M.M., at the organ. The entire seminary body from the Hong Kong Regional Seminary attended the pilgrimage, and led the community singing of hymns. Father A. Rossello of the Hong Kong Vicariate had composed music for various Chinese prayers, and this music was printed for the first time. The arrangement of the music is unique, for each Chinese monosyllabic word is arranged with music which closely approximates the actual tones of the Chinese sound of the characters. Father Rosselo was on board, and helped direct the Salesian Boys' Band and the singing of the new compositions. Hymns, of which both the words and the music were in Chinese, Latin, and English, were printed in a souvenir program; and all of these hymns were sung and resung during the Pilgrimage.

At 3:30 P.M., the Chaplain, the Rev. T. Cooney, S.J., Rector of the Hong Kong Regional Seminary, led the prayers to St. Francis Xavier, the Litany of the Blessed Mother, and the Rosary.

At 4:00 P.M., Miss Jean Armstrong lectured on *The Miracles of Goa.* This recent convert, through the intercession of St. Francis Xavier, has been cured of physical and mental trouble of long standing. Her lecture was extremely interesting, and it was enjoyed by the hundreds of passengers.

At 4:30 P.M., a sermon was given by the Most Rev. Henry Valtorta, D.D., Bishop of Hong Kong, on the subject: *Saint Francis Xavier, The Missionary*.

At 6:00 P.M., the Pilgrimage Steamer arrived at Macao, where ninety more passengers were taken aboard. At 7:00 P.M., dinner was served on board, followed by the showing of the film, *Miracles of Goa*. At 8:00 P.M., a sermon in Portuguese was delivered by the Rev. A. Sarmento, Chanter of the Macao Cathedral, followed by Portuguese prayers and hymns. At 9:00 P.M., there was congregational singing of hymns and night prayers; and, at 10:00 P.M., all retired for the night.

AT THE SANCIAN SHRINE

The following morning, at 5:00 A.M., Masses began simultaneously in different parts of the ship. Altars were set up to accommodate thirty-six priests, and many of the pilgrims received Holy Communion on the boat.

At 6:00 A.M., breakfast was served on board; and the disembarking took two hours, as the large vessel anchored about a mile from shore. Two motor-launches, *The Crusader* and *The Star of the Sea,* helped to bring the passengers to the Shrine. *The Star of the Sea* is the gift of the Rev. James F. Kelly, of Jamaica Plain, Mass., while *The Crusader* was given by the Rt. Rev. Msgr. Frank A. Thill, of Cincinnati, Ohio, Director of the *Catholic Students' Mission Crusade*. The motor-launches were aided by two large sailboats and a dozen small rowboats.

In 1932, to commemorate the 380th anniversary of the

death of St. Francis Xavier on Sancian Island, a concrete pier was built by the Maryknoll Fathers. It is two hundred feet long and eighteen feet wide, and marks the entrance to Xavier's Shrine. To this pier came the five hundred pilgrims.

At 8:00 A.M., there were prayers and private devotions at the Tomb; and, at 8:30 A.M., the Relic of Xavier was venerated by the pilgrims.

At 9:00 A.M., there was a Solemn High Mass, with the Rev. James E. McDermott, M.M., Celebrant, the Rev. Thomas A. O'Melia, M.M., Deacon, the Rev. John Heemskerk, M.M., Subdeacon, and the Rev. Bertin J. Ashness, M.M., Master of Ceremonies. The music for the Mass was furnished by the Chinese seminarians from the Regional Seminary, Aberdeen, Hong Kong. Seated in the sanctuary, near the Tomb, were: the Most Rev. James E. Walsh, M.M., D.D., Bishop of Kongmoon, in whose Vicariate Sancian Island is situated; the Most Rev. Henry Valtorta, D.D., Bishop of Hong Kong, and the Most Rev. Boniface Yeung, D.D., Auxiliary Bishop of Canton. In the few pews were seated the Rev. A. M. Sarmento, Chanter of the Macao Cathedral, Jesuits, Maryknollers, and other priests. There were ten Sisters from the Precious Blood and Maryknoll Convents at Hong Kong. All the pilgrims could not be placed within the Shrine during the Mass. The overflow was cared for by tiers of wooden seats, erected at all the windows of the church. At 10:00 A.M., outside at the natural amphitheater near Xavier's statue, the hundreds gathered to hear a sermon in Chinese delivered by the Most Rev. Boniface Yeung, Auxiliary Bishop of Canton, followed by an address of welcome by the Rev. Robert J. Cairns, M.M., Pastor of Sancian Island. The Most Rev. James E. Walsh, M.M., Bishop of Kongmoon, delivered a stirring sermon in English.

Private devotions at the Tomb and Shrine, and Stations of the Cross on the hillside above the Shrine, occupied the remainder of the time on the island until the *S.S. Haining* weighed anchor, at 2:00 P.M.

THE RETURN

On board, the prayers were led by Bishop Valtorta; hymns were sung; and an address of thanks was given by Father Cairns. Educational films of Australia and New Zealand were shown to the Chinese passengers; and a stereopticon lecture on *The Life of St. Francis Xavier* was given in Chinese by Rev. Fr. Joseph Yip of Hong Kong.

At midnight, on Sunday, December 10th, the Pilgrim Ship arrived in Hong Kong. Canton passengers spent the night on board, and returned to Canton by special car attached to the train which left Hong Kong early Monday morning. They arrived at Canton before noon.

Spiritually, this is one of the greatest events that has taken place in Far Eastern Catholic circles in many years, and we hope that St. Francis Xavier will obtain for his fervent clients many graces.

JOY ON ASH WEDNESDAY

This morning, as the rising sun began to brighten the hills behind our mission church and the birds sang sweetly in the trees of our garden, I was greeted on leaving the sacristy with the unusual and joyful sight of a crowded congregation. I had the boy count them, for I could hardly believe my eyes. "Eighty-two mouths," he said, using the Chinese expression. "Oh, let us be joyful," came to my mind immediately, and I hummed the song to myself.

Then nineteen of them went to confession (the usual Sunday congregation is less numerous than that) and two of these had not received the sacraments for years. I felt very strongly that somebody was praying hard and fervently for Sancian, for the devil certainly had a sad morning of it.

Chue Sin Shaang, a senior in the normal school at Toishan (whose way I am paying, to prepare a good teacher-catechist), is home for the New Year's vacation; and I had him read a meditation during the confessions. We have no confessional box, but instead we have a wooden screen which lifts up out of the altar railing; and the people keep away from that side of the church during confessions.

The women are separated from the men by a second altar rail, and the priest goes down to that rail during Mass to distribute Holy Communion. (Women take a back seat in China, even in church. It is an old Chinese custom.)

The ashes were blessed with the aid of incense and holy water, as prescribed by the rubrics; then the ashes were placed upon the heads of each of the eighty-two, to remind them that we are formed out of the slime of the earth and will soon return to earth.

High Mass followed. Moxie—my right-hand-man, catechist, sacristan, sexton middle-man, cook-in-a-pinch—became once more the choir. Yes, sir, the choir is a very good man.

Nineteen communions made my heart happy, and gave zest to the sermon. What an inspiration it is to look into the faces of a crowd of people. I have preached and talked to as many as two thousand at one time in my early days, when I preached in English; but never did I get such a thrill as came to me this morning. Eighty is not much of a congregation; but in Sancian where we are trying to rebuild a lost Faith, this morning's gathering was as good to me as though it had consisted of thousands.

Added to the inspiring crowd of poor fisher folk, was the fact that I was full of my subject. Ash Wednesday, Chinese New Year Day and the beginning of Lent all coincided. A new leaf, clean and white, had to be turned (and I suited action to the words by turning over a flyleaf of the missal). Last year, I said, several had ashes placed on their foreheads in this church and are now in the grave; one of us will be next. Then I told of a preacher in America who said, "Perhaps tonight"; and while he spoke, a man took sick and died in the vestibule of the church. Afterward I explained the meaning of Lent, telling them of the forty days' fast of Christ, our Model and Exemplar.

They seemed very much impressed by the fact that on Ash Wednesday in every Catholic church in the world, the same ceremony was held. It did not matter whether the congregation numbered a dozen people or a dozen thousand, or whether the people were white, black, red, yellow or brown. Everywhere the priest spoke the same words in distributing the ashes, "Remember, man, that thou art dust."

SCHOOL-FEE GOOSE

Kung hei faat choy (Happy New Year) was started well with the soul taken care of, then the fun began. The whole crowd packed into the dining room somehow, except for an overflow of the fair sex on the porch. The old men and the young kowtowed and salaamed to perfection. I had just thirteen cheap cigars, which I distributed to the men, beginning with the eldest. They all got a great "kick" out of telling their ages. The young fellows were given cigarettes, which they perhaps preferred anyway. Then to each man, woman and child were given some holy pictures and a Sacred Heart badge, with some special articles for the altar boys and catechists and servants.

When I returned to the mission residence I heard the goose "squawking," which meant that his "goose would be cooked" soon. For he was being slaughtered and would be in the pot in a few minutes. I should tell you about how we got the goose. One of our pupils in the school was unable to pay his school fee, which amounted to four Chinese dollars. At Chinese New Year, according to Chinese custom, everybody tries to pay all his bills. But the parents of our boy couldn't get hold of any money, so they wanted to know if I wouldn't please take two geese for the bill. I was delighted, and sent one ten-pounder to Bishop Walsh at Kongmoon for his large community. The other was saved for our Sancian banquet. I give the catechists and the servants a dinner on New Year's Day, and by saving the goose until today, I had a dozen pairs of chopsticks to help me dispose of the school-fee goose.

In the afternoon the tower bell called for Benediction, attended by over half a hundred "mouths." Then four good old ladies had to have rosaries, and the wee Yellow Daisies clamored for more holy pictures. Next came the dispensary work. Today there were no serious cases, I merely had to give out medicines.

The red ball of the sun was dropping behind the hills of China's mainland when I came back along the beach. As I looked across the peaceful ocean, I thought of Saint Francis Xavier who was once here looking at the same sun setting over the same ocean.

Crossing the sand-spit and the bridge, I passed our motorboat, *The Crusader,* lying in front of the house (for the tide had gone out and left her high and dry). I arrived at the church just in time for night prayers at six o'clock.

Then my meditation, prayers, spiritual reading, and rosary occupied some fruitful hours; after which I studied the Chinese Bible and another Chinese book until ten o'clock. At a quarter past eleven the chiming clock downstairs struck four beautiful notes, and since I had had such a good day, I decided to go to bed early.

VASTNESS AND FREEDOM

The sight from this porch is certainly magnificent. Besides the beauty of it, there is a great feeling of vastness and freedom from confinement which I have not heretofore enjoyed in the several missions that have previously housed my Sandy self. At Hong Kong, Yeungkong, Fachow and Sunchong, each house was in more or less confined quarters, and while commodious enough in a way, they were hemmed in on all sides by Chinese dwellings.

But now at Sancian! What a difference! Extensive grounds, long walks, the vast ocean; it is surely a delight to be at Sancian.

BARTER AND EXCHANGE

Last month we lost a *saam-paan* (three-boards) rowboat during a typhoon. The men were getting aboard the motorboat at night and, through carelessness perhaps, they lost hold and the boat was blown away towards Singapore. We never saw the "three-boards" again.

A man has been trying to sell us a boat for fifty-seven Chinese dollars, but we have refused to buy. Today we completed a deal of barter and exchange that would cause even the canniest Scotchman to sit up and take notice. We exchanged our old cow Lena for a new *saam-paan*, and thereby hangs a tale as well as a tail.

INTRODUCING LENA THE LAWN MOWER

In her childhood as a calf
She made Chinkids joke and laugh,
She was such a tiny pet.

> When they started to wean her
> She at once became leaner,
> And now she's Lena yet.

The mission at Sancian doesn't keep cows, but we kept Lena. It seems that she became so thin that even the Chinese despised her, so one day the owners brought her to the mission to eat the grass and enjoy herself. They talked to the mission dogs in passing.

What the owners of Lena said to the dogs has not been recorded, but these two guardians of the mission property are very obedient. We know only the sequel. That day the two dogs attacked Lena and made blood flow freely.

The owners then came to Father Burns, the pastor, created an awful row, yelled at the top of their voices, and threatened dire punishment to the wealthy pastor of Sancian who deprived them of the services of their valuable beast and took the rice from their mouths. Starvation and other calamities awaited them, they claimed. This continued for days. Finally Father Burns had to buy Lena and used her for a lawn mower to keep the grass cut close.

Cows in China do not give milk. I have heard it said that cows in other parts of the world do not give milk; you have to take it away from them. But in the interior of this part of China they don't have any milk that a fellow can take. As beasts of the plowshare, they are not trained as producers of milk.

A milkless, unmilkable cow is not much use, so we consider it good barter to give her away since we received in exchange a perfectly good rowboat which we need.

LIKE CHANGES TO LOVE

With the exception of trips to Hoingan to confession, and a journey one day to Hong Kong to fetch the contractor,

I have not left the island since I arrived. In the first place I have been very busy and in addition, Sancian is growing on me. I began with a liking for the place where Xavier died and gradually the liking is changing to love. From a natural and physical standpoint, Sancian Island is the best located mission that I have seen in South China. Spiritually, it does not offer much consolation in return for the effort and money expended; but what of it? Are we priests merely to enjoy the consolation that comes from the love of many devoted Catholics, or are we missioners who are willing to do our work as best we can and leave the gleaning of the harvest to future priestly generations? If a man wants merely spiritual consolations from his people, he had better not come to Sancian for a while. If he wants mission work, planting in order that others may reap, watering in order that others may store in barns, if he wants to take his place as a mere workman for the Lord of the Fields, then he is welcome here right now. Of mission work there is plenty, but the soil is often sandy or rocky or otherwise barren and requires patient cultivation. "Ours is not to reason why" this is so. "Ours is but to do and die," if necessary without the fulfillment of our dearest wishes. We can but plant and water, God gives the increase.

And in zealous work, in the remembrance of Xavier's *"Da mihi animas,"* we hope to intensify our love for Sancian Island.

BELATED VOCATIONS

Father Vieban, the eminent Sulpician at Saint Mary's Seminary, Baltimore, once told me: "If I had my way, every seminarian would be obliged to spend three years in the world. We would lose some, but we would have only the good ones left."

When I was ordained, I was within a few months of my 34th birthday. As a matter of fact, on the missions, age doesn't seem to be a hindrance to getting the language or to adapting oneself to the new conditions of life. Personally, I think it is rather a help. For at 35 a man is settled, does his work without prodding, and on the whole does creditable work. Father Gonnet, S.J., who started the activities of the Jesuits in Shanghai over a century ago, wrote to his superiors in France that he wanted older men, about 35 years of age.

Mission work here in China is difficult. It requires strong faith and a right good will. But anyone with good health, ordinary intelligence, and zeal for souls can carry on and become a good missioner. It means much sacrifice; but love of God is measured by sacrifice. The more we suffer in parting with dear ones, the more we show our love for Him.

SUNRISE ON SANCIAN

At half past four this morning, I started out the door, and was greeted by our Chinese dog, Nigger. It was so dark that I couldn't see him, until I felt his tongue licking my hands. Then from out of the inky blackness came a voice: *"Teen Chue po yow Shen Fu."* (God bless you, Father.) And upon inquiry, I found that the Chinese cook was scraping the scales from some tiny fish, preparatory to cooking them for the Chinese servants and catechists.

"Why, you can't see a thing," I said to him. "No, but I can feel the fish," he replied. So I left him feeling the fish, and with flashlight in hand, started on my walk along the narrow, winding path skirting a village and going over the top of the hill to the other side of the island. The hilly path is steep and narrow, and made by hundreds of stones, more or less flat, laid to resemble a flight of stairs. But the steps are unequal in height and length and width, so I had to keep the flashlight constantly in use ascending the hill. But when I had reached the top (puffing like a steam engine), it began to be light enough to see the path.

Over the top, there was a sight to gladden the eyes. The vista for several miles to the ocean is ordinarily a beautiful sight from this point. But instead of the usual magnificent view, in the dim light nothing could be seen of the detailed outlines. What struck my eyes was the galaxy of lights spread below me, grouped here and there across the vast lowlands. Later, I found out that I was watching fishermen, who by lantern light were catching a special fish that abounds in the streams just before dawn.

When I had reached the bottom of the hill, it was very bright; because here in the Orient, the day comes suddenly, and disappears just as quickly. It is almost like the raising and dropping of a curtain. Then I made speed, and got myself into a fine state of perspiration, walking as fast as I could to my destination. Just before I reached there, the ball of fire rose out of the ocean, and the red reflection on the blue waves was worth coming miles to see. I shall not soon forget that magnificent sunrise.

I reached the chapel at Sai Ngau Peng (Western Cow Plains) at six o'clock, heard six confessions, said Mass and then examined twenty-one boys in catechism.

Last of all came Mary Leung, seventy-nine, crippled, and deaf. What for? "To go to confession, Father. I haven't been for over ten years, and I want to make my peace with God." She did that.

Do you wonder that I walked back the four miles rejoicing? Please, will you pray that we find some more Mary Leungs on Sancian Island.

A DAY ON THE MISSIONS

"What do you do all day?" asked someone in a recent letter. Here is a record of today's events. At 6 A.M. we said the Angelus and morning prayers at the main mission church for the schoolboys, teachers and a few Christians. We left them praying, and accompanied by the cook and the houseboy, who carried a table, vestments, a chalice, hosts, wine and everything necessary for Mass, we walked to *Taai Long Waan* (Great Waves Harbor), a village half an hour away.

There in the chapel we heard the confession of one blind woman, a real saint. Mass was attended by about twenty schoolboys and one man from the village, as well as by those who had come from the mission with us. Two catechists could see to come to the stone step before the altar; but the woman who has lost her eyesight remained kneeling on her straw matting and devoutly received Holy Communion. We wish we had her simple faith. After Mass, we preached to our one devoted Catholic in Great Waves Harbor. She is not blind to the things that count, for she knows better than her fellow villagers the value of her soul. The man and the schoolboys listened attentively.

SANCIAN'S FIRST CATHOLIC

This village was once a thriving seat of Catholicity, but "some of the seed fell on stony ground"—in fact, nearly all of it. The cause? No one but God knows. The poor people were admitted to baptism with meagre instruction, perhaps, for our French predecessors did not have enough catechists. And all the people of this village were made Catholics at one general roundup. If their faith is weak, it may be the fault of no one; very possibly it is merely God's way of showing us what poor instruments we are to act as His agents and missioners. Besides, it is not easy to become a Catholic in China; and it is much more difficult to remain a true follower of Christ. The new converts are criticized and often ostracized by their fellow villagers, and even by the members of their own family.

On the hill behind the mission house is buried Mr. Lam, the first Catholic of Sancian Island, and an example of such a convert. Not only were his beginnings difficult, but during later persecutions he stood up for the Faith, sacrificed much, and persevered until the end, an abused, misunderstood, loyal, stanch Catholic. Such are the foundation stones upon which we build.

But to get back to the "stony ground" in the village of "Great Waves." The Faith there is nearly dead. We had hoped to revive it by repairing the chapel as the first step. The orphans at Macao made the windows, but the depression in our funds has made it impossible for us to hire laborers to put them in place. Many roof tiles are missing; there is not a door or window in the church. The catechist's house next to the memorial chapel has also been visited by marauders and thieves who have gradually stolen the doors, the stairway, the upper floor and the beams. They have even started stealing the roof tiles from this house as well as from the chapel. The stealing is still going on, though we hope to save what remains of the buildings until we can get enough to repair them.

Five hundred American dollars would do the trick; but in these days of the depression even five dollars is a lot of money, with so many out of work, living from hand to mouth, losing their homes, and suffering terribly. So we do not hope to reroof the chapel for a long time. Some day, when God wants the chapel repaired, He will tell some good soul to send us a little something for this need.

FRIENDLY PAGANS

Walking home alone through Great Waves Harbor we conversed with several of the villagers, who seem very friendly; some even invited us to dine with them. The school there has about forty pupils. The teacher, Yip Sin Shaang, is trying to arrange with the village elders to allow us to send a catechist to teach doctrine to the boys. In the children is our great hope. Please keep this in your prayers.

We were back at the central mission at nine, to partake of our save-for-the-missions breakfast.

MENU

CEREAL, Rice.
EGGS, Fried. Both of them.
TOAST, Dry.
BEVERAGE, Tea.

We made a round of the property to see that the workmen were on the job and had them bring *"The Crusader,"* our motorboat, to the front door, which is our dry dock. Now they are filling the cracks with *Paak-fooi-yau* (white-lime-oil), a Chinese concoction a trifle harder than our putty. This has to be done to both pilgrimage motorboats twice a year. *"The Crusader,"* is now leaking, but it will be O.K. in a couple of days.

In the garden, we saw that our "Vegetable-King" planted and watered a few more vegetables, in order to prepare against the coming of priest visitors during the summer.

OUR BLESSED MOTHER'S MONTH

May devotions were at high noon, which seems most convenient for the Chinese, midway between their two-meals-a-day. The sermon on our Blessed Mother was followed by Benediction. The four altar boys learning to serve Benediction were given another instruction and drill in the Benediction ceremonies.

In the dispensary, after the noon devotions, we treated colds and fevers, ulcers and boils, headache and "heartache," (a Chinese expression for "something wrong inside," and it may be anything), and we distributed pills for ills galore.

Lunch and a nap during the heat of the tropical day; a visit to the Blessed Sacrament; spiritual reading from the "Early Years of St. Jerome"; a chapter of the Bible; the reading of the Breviary; night prayers with the Christians; and Chinese study brought us to suppertime, seven o'clock. Towards the end of the frugal meal (soup, fish, rice and greens from our garden, dry bread and tea) the four catechists were invited to *yam c'ha*, which means a little more than "drink tea" for we shared with them some cakes that the cook had provided. We made a visit to the chapel, while the dishes were being cleared away; then played a game of chess with a catechist (whom we taught to beat us), while the other teachers and several employees made an audience.

GOD GIVES THE HARVEST

A short walk on the tennis court; a conference with Mok Sin Shaang, our 'number one' catechist; another with Ah Kay, our cook-sailor, about the boats; the saying of the

Rosary; and then we go to our room. But not to bed; for this is when we get in our best licks at bookkeeping, mission plans and writing; so instead of sleeping right away, we are writing these lines. It's now eleven o'clock at night, and we're good for another hour or two.

Even an ordinary day on the missions is full of interest and replete with consolations; for when working for God, who counts only the effort and energy expended, we do not have to produce results in the souls of those whom we try to reach. He does that. And the time when He will give the grace to fallen-aways and pagans lies entirely in His hands. Ours is the duty to "preach in season and out of season." Conversions are given only in accordance with His Divine decrees; the Holy Spirit moves hearts when and where He wills.

FACE TO FEET

Kwan Kwok Chow, whom we called *Ah Fuk* ("Happiness"), had not had many happy occasions in his life. Originally from Yeungkong, this widowed man and his son drifted to Sancian years ago and lived in an abandoned house near Great Waves Harbor.

When Fr. Constantine Burns, of Toledo, O., was made Pastor of Sancian he had with him for a time Brother John Dorsey, a graduate nurse whose ministrations to the poor and afflicted brought people here from every part of the Island. I still constantly get echoes of his many acts of kindness. Among others who were attracted to the mission was "Happiness," who had for years suffered from elephantiasis. The disease had made him a pitiable sight, and the right side of his face hung down nearly a foot, so that his ear was at chin-level. Brother John, in his characteristic way, rechristened him "Face to Feet," and the name stuck with him; at the same time Brother did what he could to cure the poor man, but his ailment had been let go for too long a time. Father Burns did more, for he took him into the mission and charitably provided him with food and a place in which to sleep.

Later "Happiness" Junior, the little "Lamb," also came to the mission, and, though neither did much work, they had a home and were assured of a living such as it was.

Last month, "Happiness" took ill, and the local doctor did what he could for him. But the patient was beyond the care of even the best of doctors.

On August twenty-sixth, we performed the last act of charity for "Happiness" on this earth, paid for burial clothes and a coffin, had funeral services in the church, and accompanied his remains to the grave on "Holy Hill." Dear "Happiness," in this earthly life of ours you had very little happiness, but now your body is lifeless from "face to feet" and your soul is in Heaven enjoying real Happiness, which will never end.

SANCIAN HOLY WEEK

Our few "Chinkids" from the school had been trained for the ceremony of Holy Thursday, and we had a white candle ready for each of the thirty chubby right hands. The twenty-nine boys and one girl were to march in Procession with the Blessed Sacrament from here to the Shrine of Saint Francis Xavier, where hours of work had produced a Repository on a table, and though the Repository-on-the-table would perhaps not have won great commendation from *Liturgical Arts,* yet it was as well done as could be with available materials. The Tabernacle was veiled in silk, clean linen cloths hid the table, and the whole was banked with flowers including roses from our blooming garden. It was a beautiful Repository!

But the North Wind came Holy Thursday and blew so strong, with pelting rain and roaring waves, that it was impossible to have the outdoor Procession. Not only that, but most of the expected congregation did not show up, for there were only thirteen schoolboys, the one lone schoolgirl, one faithful man and *Moxie* and his family. So we hurriedly made a Repository at the side altar of the Sacred Heart, used paper flowers, makeshift vases and candlesticks (for all had been prepared at Xavier's Shrine), and carried on. Instead of men canopy-bearers we had boys. Wrinkled Old Lam, whose surname means *forest,* was the lone tree as he held aloft the purple-veiled Tree of the Cross at the head of the Procession. He was followed by the few people, each bearing a flaming candle, and finally came the acolytes, the censer-bearers, the canopy, and Our Divine Lord Himself in the Hidden Sacred Host. The ceremonies were just as pleasing to Our Lord, I hope, as were those at Notre Dame in Paris. When typhoons blow it is a brave boy who stirs from his *wee clay hoose.*

Later we sent to Xavier's Shrine for the vases, flowers, and candlesticks and adorned our Repository more ornately; then all of us took turns in Adoration of our God of Love in the Most Blessed Sacrament.

Good Friday brought better weather, only a drizzling rain and not so strong a wind; we had about thirty for the Procession and the Mass of the Presanctified. At noon the Pastor led his few faithful along the *Via Crucis,* stopping at each Station for a Chinese meditation and prayer.

Holy Saturday was still biting cold and windy. We had half-an-hour's delay in making the new fire from the flint and steel, but, with the Chinese patience which we seem to have acquired, we finally succeeded. The forty-two on-lookers saw the triple-candle being lighted, and genuflected at the singing of the words: *"Lumen Christi, Deo Gratias."* Forty-two onlookers saw the blessing of the Paschal Candle, with its Cross inlaid by five grains of incense. Forty-two patient listeners heard the long prophecies read, the Litany sung, and the Mass celebrated.

Easter Sunday, despite the cold wind and rain, there were exactly fifty-six men and boys and thirty-four women and girls, a total of eighty at High Mass, and sixteen of these received Holy Communion. The four altar boys in white served High Mass like old timers.

FATHER SONGBIRD

After the Chinese were asleep the two of us went on deck where we said our rosary together; then, as we watched the phosphorescence of the South China Sea, we broke into song. Father Cleary's every note is perfect and his throat is a songbird's. He took a great fancy to the chorus of a song composed by my Glasgow cousin, Tommy Ferrie: *"We're all toddling down the brae."*

Singing it made me think of my Mother. She cannot read a note of music nor play an instrument, yet she can entertain listeners by the hour with long Scotch and Irish songs, the words and music of which are stored up in that once prodigious memory of hers. I can hear her now singing, *"Mother Machree."* What are a mere ten thousand miles between me and my "Mother Machree"? "My eyes is . . . my eyes is . . . my eyes is leakin', be blamed if they ain't."

Father Patrick Cleary, who knows his musical sharps and flats as a Scotch greengrocer knows his spinach and onions, commanded that Tommy Ferrie do up in his very best Scotch for Korean consumption the words and music of *"Toddling Down."* The Maryknoll songbird from Ithaca also ordered that a publisher be found for the song. If you happen to be toddling down by Tommy's door in Glasgow, please give him this message from Father Songbird.

CHRISTMAS COMES TO SANCIAN

Figures for our Sancian Crib were sent by Patrick Lennon, a poor Irish soldier. They arrived in the nick of time, on Christmas Eve. The Crib went the rounds to five different places, where I explained its meaning to the children. It was fun to see the little yellow faces peering into the box we used for a cave, and it was good to watch their almond eyes twinkle as they answered my questions: "That Baby is Jesus." "The Lady is *Shing Mo Ma-Lei-A* (Mary)."

Before the Midnight Mass I went through the neighboring village of *San-Tei* (New Earth), playing the mandolin and singing, *"Adeste Fideles, Venite Adoremus."* Then the church tower bell awakened those who had not heard my caroling.

I walked towards the path to the Memorial Shrine, only to find that it was covered by the high tide and therefore impassable. My brother's Worcester canoe had also arrived on Christmas Eve, so we put it on our shoulders and christened it by launching it on the briny deep. The moon was shining brightly upon the silvery, shimmering waves, the paddles brought forth the golden phosphorescence that lies hidden in our waters; and, as the canoe moved Shrinewards, I played the mandolin and the choristers and I sang Christmas carols.

MIDNIGHT MASS AT THE XAVIER SHRINE

At the tomb where the Apostle of the Orient was first buried, High Mass was sung by the pastor, Father "Sandy" Cairns, of Glasgow, Scotland, Worcester, Mass., Maryknoll, N. Y., and Sancian.

The Gospel for Midnight Mass, telling of the shepherds who left their night watches to adore the Baby Jesus, was truly re-enacted by the few brave souls who dared to climb Xavier's hill at midnight. Eight received in Holy Communion their Infant King and Savior.

After Mass I was edified by the devotion shown by the faithful few at the Crib. It had been set up in a box under a pine tree sprinkled with cotton snowflakes, and a flashlight, hidden in the upper recesses of the box, brought out in strong relief the tiny figure of the Divine Infant.

DAWN MASS AT THE CENTRAL MISSION

The Daylight Mass was sung in Sancian's parish church, and sixteen received Holy Communion. Among them were two who had returned to the Fold after a long absence from the Sacraments.

Sixteen is a small number out of more than a thousand former Catholics on the Island, but the others will return if and when God gives them the grace. A crusade of prayer is the lodestone needed to draw down on this Sacred Spot of the Orient, now barren and desolate, the life-giving Pentecostal flame.

After Mass, the children were made happy with candy and holy pictures, and the men with tobacco.

NOON MASS AT GREAT WAVES HARBOR

Shortly before noon, the third High Mass of Christmas Day was sung at *Taai Long Waan,* Great Waves Harbor, where Mary Lam, a grandmother (whom we call our blind saint), is our only practicing Catholic. The others have reverted to paganism.

However, the pastor, mandolin-a-strumming, with his

choristers went through the village on the way to the church singing Christmas hymns. The boys followed in motley array with the organ, a picture of Our Lady of Lourdes, a table and the other necessities for Mass, including a new set of white Mass vestments recently sent by a charitable Sister in New York City. The Christians from our Central Mission carried kneeling benches, which served for seats as well.

The impromptu procession attracted fully a hundred, who heard a Christmas sermon and attended High Mass in a windowless, doorless and partly roofless mud church.

The choir, Johnny Lau and Joe Yau, for the first time in their lives sang for three High Masses on the same day, and although they would not be selected as soloists by Saint Patrick's Cathedral in New York, yet they sang the Masses quite well and are now proud of their achievement.

Benediction at the Central Mission was followed by a Chinese Christmas turkey (pork) dinner for the catechists and servants, at which banquet the pastor presided.

It was indeed a very happy Christmas.

WHAT DIFFERENCE DOES IT MAKE?

As we look back on the year we can find no great cause for rejoicing at the spiritual progress of Sancian's people. We had no Baptisms, though we did have a few return to the Sacraments.

At all events we have done the best we could, leaving the results to God.

And if visible results here and now are meager, what difference does it make? We are sticking to our post. Besides, at this beautiful mission so well situated on the ridge of the ocean, I have the great privilege of being Custodian of the Shrine and Tomb of Saint Francis Xavier.

I'm as happy as the day is long; and when you read this I shall be getting happier, because the days will be getting longer.

A BARRAGE OF QUESTIONS

This morning as I was walking along the sands and rocks to the shrine of Xavier, four young girls caught up with me and though I had my rosary in my hand, they couldn't let a little thing like that bother them. They wanted to talk to the *Shen Fu* and they did. In fact, they accompanied me right to the pier at the entrance to the shrine, where they started their morning labor of picking up greens which later they would feed to the pigs—greens left clinging to the stones by the ebbing tide. It was such an unusual thing in China to have girls walk with a man, especially on Sancian, that I knew they must have an important reason for doing so. They did. In their young minds, the most important thing in their lives was the announcement that I made last Sunday at Mass: "The Maryknoll Sisters are coming to Sancian."

What a barrage of questions! "Who? what? when? where? why?" didn't begin to cover their spirited questionnaire. I had told my Sunday congregation that the Sisters would be on the island before many months had passed. During my four years here I have been unable to do much with the girls and women, and have talked to the Sisters in Hong Kong several times, asking "When?" But it took a visit to Sancian by "the big shots," including the Hong Kong Number One, to make the coming of Sister-helpers definite. So my Robinson Crusoe days will soon be over; and by the same token ladies of Sancian will soon be flocking to the Church, I hope. The Sisters are going to live in an old Chinese mud-house, and do some pioneering. Please pray for them and for me.

SISTERS AHOY!

A few moons ago, there came to Sancian Island where St. Francis Xavier died a boatload of canaries, doves and ducklings. In among them was a pair of Maryknoll Sisters.

I told the new missioner arrivals that my Robinson Crusoe five years on the island had ended; and Sister replied: "Yes, Father, now you have two Fridays."

My main concern is to fix the Sisters as comfortably as possible in the poor Chinese house which they abuse with the name *Convent*. It is low-roofed, attracting the terrific heat in the tropical summer; during the rainy season, the house has had a foot of water on the ground floor. I have had the house covered with a hired matshed which costs thirty Chinese dollars a month, and a stone trench is being built around the *Convent* to lead torrential rain waters to the ocean. The contract for the trench and the digging of a well demands two hundred and ten Chinese dollars. Although I am a Scot, I throw every piece of spare cash I can get hold of into the ditch or the well.

The Sancian personnel increased by two hundred per cent is an event worthy of notice. The pastor is delighted to have the Sisters here to try and win the souls of the women and girls of Xavier's Isle. Now we number three, each born in a different country: a Portuguese, an American, and a Scot. The three nationalities are under the one Maryknoll Banner and one Standard of the Cross as we try to win more souls for Jesus Christ.

Sister Candida Maria Basto is from Hong Kong. She speaks Chinese fluently. Being a musician of ability, she has taken over Sancian's organist duties and is now half the choir. The other half, Sister Monica Marie Boyle, of Pottsville, Penna., is a trained nurse. She is a valuable addition to the Sancian personnel, because we hope by scientific medical work to win the hardened Sancian-ites.

Visiting the villages, the Sisters are already making contacts with the women and girls. The Sisters feel, as I do, that it is a privilege of the highest order to be selected to work on Xavier's Isle.

"THE DUMB CATECHIST"

For four years I have been the pastor of Sancian Island and the custodian of the shrine church which covers the tomb of Saint Francis Xavier.

Since 1552, when Xavier became a saint by his death on this island in the South China Sea, Sancian has been a place of renown and a spot revered by lovers of the greatest missionary since the time of Jesus Christ and the Apostles.

Unfortunately, however, the missionary work on this sacred isle has been rather difficult and productive of meager results. Recently I was able to write, "I have not had an adult conversion during my four years at Sancian." But now I can say that no longer. "Old Yellow" (Lo Wong) has been baptized and is now Francis Xavier Wong. The "Dumb Catechist" is to blame for it.

Here's how it happened. The writer, Father Sandy, is a doctor of parts. He learned most of his medical knowledge from his good Scottish Mother who had a thriving practice with her eleven children, seven of whom (including Sandy) were born in Scotland and the other four were "made in America." Father Sandy also studied "first aid" and the fundamentals of medicine under Dr. Flagg at Maryknoll, New York. With this wonderful (?) medical education, Father Sandy runs a dispensary at the mission at Sancian, and a street dispensary every Sunday after a Mass in the public street in Saam Chow Kaai (Three Islands Street Market).

THE WINNING OF ''OLD YELLOW''

A call came to the dispensary. "Old Yellow" Wong was very sick and wanted Father Sandy to come and see him. Which Father Sandy did. "Old Yellow" had been an enemy of the mission, and had caused trouble for Father Sandy and the Catholic Church on several occasions. But when a call comes from a fellow on the flat of his back, a priest goes. Father Sandy went.

For six days previous to my visit, the poor old fellow had eaten practically nothing. He had no desire to eat, nor even to live, and his relatives were sure that he would die within a day or two. I gave the poor old man some medicine; and I saw that food was the best medicine that I could give him. But he couldn't eat. Fresh milk was sent to him three times a day, every time we could take any away from the cow. Old Wong began to improve; bran and milk made him sit up and take notice. He walked to church Easter Sunday, the first time during my years here that he was ever inside the Catholic church.

He is now baptized and it is entirely due to our "Dumb Catechist." The first man, woman or child who sends ten dollars for a month's upkeep of our "Dumb Catechist" and her brother Bull, will have a high place in the list of Sancian's benefactors.

You may address your check to

Father Sandy, (R.J. Cairns)
Sancian Island,
Kwong Hoi, Canton, China.

September 1, 1936.

This appeal of Father Robert J. Cairns, M.M., has my hearty approval. . . . Father Cairns is fighting an uphill battle in the toughest mission that I ever saw in my eighteen years in China, and any help given to him to assist his heroic efforts for his backward people ought to receive a special blessing from God.

J. E. Walsh (Vic. Apost. of Kongmoon, China)

ORIENTAL EASTER

Polite Chinese people invite even travelers to "Eat rice before you start home," or say, "Spend the night with us and take your long homeward walk slowly tomorrow morning." But if you suddenly took them at their word, they would be surprised, and perhaps embarrassed by a shortage of beds and food. Therefore men "in the know" make the usual reply, "Don't trouble yourself," and continue on their way.

Perhaps it is because of the "polite language" invitations, that Chinese etiquette requires three invitations to be issued if you really want someone to come to your place for a meal or an overnight stay.

So four weeks before Easter the first invitations were delivered to the distant village elders by the gardener, the cowboy, and the caretaker, who took the pastor's card to each village. A week later the second invitations, written on red paper, were delivered by the higher-ups (the catechists). The third invitations were delivered by the missioner himself during the following week.

More than three hundred people came, although our small church has a capacity for only one-third that number. The High Mass began at nine o'clock.

Here, the women sit at the back of the church; their husbands and sons are at the front, separated by a railing running across the church. At this lower railing the women receive Holy Communion. And, since the church is a place of rest as well as of devotion, the women untie the bundles of children from their backs and let the youngsters play on the church floor. They are a distraction to Westerners, but the Chinese have been doing that from time immemorial and are so accustomed to it that baby noises in church never bother them.

After Mass the pastor sat in with his three hundred and fifty guests for a Chinese banquet. Thirty-five tables had been prepared; but, since we had only a few actual tables, the great majority sat down on the grass in circles of ten, with their rice bowls and chopsticks in their hands and the meats and vegetables in the center of each group of people. Each circle on the grass was one "table."

At two o'clock all was over, and the people started for their long walk home, which for some of them meant three hours of climbing up one mountain and down another.

At five o'clock a large group of Catholics assembled for night prayers, and afterwards they gave the official count: 187 had fitted into the church, 368 had been fed, eight new villages were represented, people were here from twenty-six pagan villages.

"Blessed be God!" said the pastor as he took up his Breviary and fell sound asleep.

RICE AND OLD SHOES

I have been on the staff of the Canton International Red Cross, operating in the refugee areas of South China, since November, 1938. Here is a glimpse of what the Committee has been doing:

With over 2,000 in four camps, some 75,000 meals have been served every day from 26 feeding centers. Each week 10,000 dispensary cases were treated; 50,000 quinine pills were distributed in one month; 30,000 inoculations were given against cholera and smallpox, and some 5,000 patients were placed in Government institutions. Six hospitals and several staffs of doctors were required to meet the urgent medical needs of the sick and injured, and 500 tons of cracked wheat (sent by the people of the United States) were exhausted in no time. Since the end of January, 1939, conditions have materially changed; but the price of rice is going up daily, and unless help is forthcoming we face a serious situation.

The work has been extremely interesting and, to my mind, one of the most important opportunities that the Catholic Church in South China has had. To have Catholic priests on both the Red Cross Executive Committee and on the Refugee Committee was a new departure in Canton. To have the Refugee Office in the priest's house, where it was visited daily by many missioners of all nations and denominations, was an unusual thing for this section of China. But there was a splendid spirit of cooperation manifested by all, who pulled together like a well-trained crew in the great emergency. The Red Cross has done a mighty good job in Canton, and I am proud to have had a little share in it.

Another feature of relief was the "Old-Shoe Party" which I arranged among the foreign children of Canton. The children collected 984 pairs of shoes to be distributed to poor Chinese men, women, and children.

The "Old-Shoe Party" had its culmination on a recent afternoon in the Canton Club. The affair was enjoyed by fifty-two children. An entertainment of magic and music preceded the tea party and the awarding of prizes. Prizes were awarded the children for their efforts in collecting footwear. The first prize went to Marie Prata, who had gathered 350 pairs of shoes. Next came Ani Gomez with a record of 214 pairs. Kathleen Farrell, third, had 116 pairs; and Teresa Baptista, fourth, had 105.

Plans were made to make the "Old-Shoe Party" an annual event during the Christmas holidays.

BACK FROM CANTON

On Sundays I go out to the villages and Father Joyce preaches at the mission. At the pagan village of Ch'a Waan (Tea Harbor), which Father Joyce calls "Boston," I gave out medicines and clothes on March 23rd and the people were grateful. They were to be busy fishing Sunday morning and some of the men couldn't come to Mass, so they asked me to preach at night.

They arranged logs, benches and board seats in the public square, hung a lamp on a high bamboo tripod and over two hundred fishermen gathered to hear me. I read the Gospel, and from the words of our Lord showed them the advantages of believing in Jesus Christ.

Catechist Leung Yuk Man, who with his family has a house in "Boston," followed my reading with an excellent sermon and kept the people at attention for half an hour.

I'm now singing:

> "Gee, ain't it great to be home
> Back with your friends, once more?
> No more I'm going to roam
> Upon a foreign shore."

breathless early morning hours of his priest-hood; the heavy weariness of late nights at the Yeung Kong mission, at Fachow, at Sunchong; the heartbreak in Canton among the war sufferers and refugees; the uphill, heavy climb against the paganism of Sancian Island, where Francis Xavier had died.

All the memories were softened by the flow of his own good humor, by the smile that won him easy entrance into the hearts of his people and his fellow priests. THREE DAYS TO ETERNITY records the joys and sorrows of these memories, and most of all the rollicking lightheartedness of this soldier of Christ.

About The Authors...

Richard Reid, noted editor and lawyer, was born in Winchester, Mass. He was educated at the Academy of the Sacred Heart, Holy Cross College, Worcester, Mass., Columbia and Fordham Universities.

Since 1940 Mr. Reid has been editor of *The Catholic News* of the New York Archdiocese. He had served earlier on the *Augusta (Ga.) Chronicle*, and the *Augusta Herald*. From 1920 to 1940 he was editor of *The Bulletin* and executive secretary of the Catholic Layman's Association of Georgia.

Mr. Reid has been honored as a Knight of St. Gregory and a Knight of the Holy Sepulchre. In 1936 he received the Laetare Medal from Notre Dame and in 1946 the Hoey Medal for Interracial Justice.

Father Edward J. Moffett was born in Newark, N. J., on February 11, 1922. After his ordination in 1948 he labored as a missioner in China, visiting many of the places where Father Cairns had labored earlier. Father Moffett was imprisoned twice by the Chinese Reds, and eventually expelled from the mainland of China after having been first sentenced by a "People's Court" to be executed.